TURN THE

Turn the Page

A Southern Chick's Memoir

Michelle Blair

This is non-fiction; however, some names and circumstances have been changed to protect the identity of individuals.

Copyright ©

Copyright © 2024 by Michelle Blair

All rights reserved, no part of this book may be reproduced or used in any manner without written permission of the copyright owner except for the use of quotations in a book review.

ISBN-13-9798883603333

This book is dedicated to:

Benjamin Eli Harris, who taught me how to love.

I Love you not only for what you are,

but for what I am when I am with you.

I Love You, Benny

Contents

- CHAPTER 1 THE PUZZLE ... 1
- CHAPTER 2 SEEKING JUSTICE ... 13
- CHAPTER 3 CANDY CRUSH ... 21
- CHAPTER 4 CANDLEWOOD ... 27
- CHAPTER 5 THE NEW GIRL ... 35
- CHAPTER 6 KEEPER OF THE NISHIKIGOI ... 41
- CHAPTER 7 FORTUNATE ONE ... 51
- CHAPTER 8 QUE SERA SERA ... 57
- CHAPTER 9 THE CARDINAL RULE ... 63
- CHAPTER 12 BLACK SQUIRRELS ... 81
- CHAPTER 13 BENNY ... 89
- CHAPTER 14 THE DAY I DIED ... 99
- CHAPTER 15 MAMA DON'T LEAVE ME ... 105
- CHAPTER17 BECOMING AN EAGLE ... 123
- CHAPTER 18 JUROR NUMBER NINE ... 127
- CHAPTER 19 THAT'S THE WAY LOVE GOES ... 133
- CHAPTER 20 TAKE OFF YOUR GRAVE CLOTHES ... 137
- CHAPTER 21 AGAINST THE WIND ... 141
- ACKNOWLEDGEMENTS ... 175
- AUTHOR BIOGRAPHY ... 177

PROLOGUE

I was being pressured every way. We met at the baseball field and discussed the problem but came up with no solution. So, during the talk I left and felt if I could get away from all of it, I could have time to think. No one knew I took Michelle and some clothes, and we came to Charlotte. We got a motel room at Travel-lodge under my name. I was there one day and two nights. My mind was in great turmoil about what I needed to do. I could not live under the strain of all the talk and accusations.

TURN THE PAGE

You can listen to the engine

Moaning out his one note song

You can think about the woman

Or the girl you knew the night before

But your thoughts will soon be wandering

The way they always do

When you're riding sixteen hours

And there's nothing much to do

And you don't feel like much like riding

You just wish the trip was through

Here I am

On the road again

There I am

Up on the stage

Here I am

Playing the Star again

There I go Turn the Page

Well, you walk into a restaurant

Strung out from the road

And you feel the eyes upon you

As you're shaking off the cold

You pretend it doesn't bother you

But you just want to explode

Most times you can't hear em talk

Other times you can

All the same old cliches

Is that a woman or a man?

And you always seem outnumbered

You don't dare make a stand

Here I am

On the road again

There I am

Up on the stage

Here I go

Playing the Star again There I go

Turn the page

Out there in the spotlight

You're a million miles away

Every ounce of energy

You try to give away

As the sweat pours out your body

Like the music that you play

Later in the evening

As you lie awake in bed

With the echoes of the amplifiers

Ringing in your head

You smoke the day's last cigarette

Remembering what she said

Here I am

On the road again

On a long and lonesome highway

East of Omaha

There I am

Up on the stage

Here I go

Playing the star again

There I go

Turn the Page

Here I am

On the road again

There I am

Up on the stage

Here I go

Playing the star again

There I go

There I go

Bob Seger

CHAPTER 1 THE PUZZLE

My earliest memories were the beginning of a puzzle I still piece together to this day. It was the sixties-one of the most tumultuous times in history marked by the Civil Rights Movement, the Vietnam War, Political Assassinations, and a younger generation that pushed boundaries by experimenting with psychedelic drugs, free love, promiscuous sex, and Rock N Roll. Me and my baby brother, Michael, lived in Charlotte, NC, with my mom, Nancy, or Nancy Kate as she was called. In the South, often people had either two names or nicknames. The South has its own rules and traditions. In Charlotte-" the Queen City" Scotch-Irish immigrants conveyed along the Great Wagon Road from Philadelphia. King George III ruled the colonies when the town was chartered in 1768. It was named after his wife; Queen Charlotte and the county paid homage to her birthplace in Germany which was Mecklenburg. Old Nation's Path was a trading route for Native American Indians, mostly Catawba Indians. My great ancestor, Hezekiah Alexander was a signer of the Declaration of Mecklenburg which preempted the Declaration of Independence. Hezekiah Alexander's house still stands and is now a museum. It was built in 1774. Charlotte earned the nickname "Hornet's Nest" when General Cornwallis was chased out of the city by a swarm of hornets in the Revolutionary War.

On the weekends we visited Robin, Kerry, and Kevin-my older brothers-and Grandma Kate or "Mama Kate." It does not sound right to visit your brothers and it did not feel right either. They lived in the town of Ansonville, NC, which was about an hour away as the crow flies. Ansonville had a beautiful, pastoral setting with cotton fields that stretched out like white sea foam, cow pastures where cows and horses grazed lazily, there was corn and tobacco as far as the eye could see. Honeysuckle bushes, blackberries, raspberries, and pecan trees were all around, their scent clinging in the air. Ansonville was named after George Anson, a First Baron British Admiral that watched over the Navy during the Seven Years War. In the Piedmont Region, Anson County was originally vast. Rowan, Mecklenburg, Union, and Montgomery counties were once Anson County. The Pee Dee River stretched throughout the county and often flooded. The land was green with hills and the dirt looked like red clay. The Town of Wadesboro was not only the county seat, but it was the place where Andrew Jackson was issued his license to practice law. I missed my brothers something terrible and I couldn't remember for the life of me why we weren't together. I guess they didn't know either. No one was allowed to talk about it. My life was filled with secrets, and I hated them. Secrets never did make any sense to me and when I grew up, I would make sure there were no secrets. No secrets allowed. I couldn't even remember my dad and wasn't supposed to mention his name, which was Buddy Martin. His real name was James Kenneth Martin, but everyone called him "Buddy." All I knew for sure was Robin, Kerry and Kevin lived with him, and he was a cowboy. They helped him work on his ranch and I guess I didn't matter to him because I would not be much help-being a girl and all. Somewhere deep inside, I longed to be a part of it all. Nancy Kate never talked about Buddy. In fact, Nancy Kate never really talked about anything important, but she did talk all the time. She was an only child and loved to be the center of attention. Nancy Kate was a whirlwind of bright clothes, deep blue eyeshadow, and swooping hair. Hairspray was a powerful thing back then. She was a good mother-always took care of us when we were sick and was a wonderful cook, but she was childlike-a paradox of love. I knew from an early age that I would have to take care of her, and since Michael was a baby, I would take care of him too. Nancy Kate wasn't quite right in the head, but I was not sure if she would grow out of it or not. She worked hard and tried her best. We lived in a little white house on the corner of Attaberry Street. At the time, this was in a rough neighborhood. Nancy Kate worked diligently at Eckerd Drug Store's home office where her secret battles were hidden behind a secretary's desk. She was exceptionally good at her job and never missed work. I went to weekday school at Plaza Presbyterian Church. It was formed in 1907 and had a Gothic Revival style. The benches, worn smooth overtime, witnessed prayers whispered and hopes shared. Somehow the Fellowship Hall met up with the big church which was surrounded by colorful stained-glass windows. It seemed the perfect place to pray and honor God. Nancy Kate was in the choir and acted in plays. She loved to sing and act. On Sundays, Nancy Kate would sing in the choir, Michael would be in church nursery, and I would sit with Mrs. Wheeler. She was a sweet little old lady with a crown of white hair. After singing, giving money, and saying a verse, the Preacher would start his half a day long sermon- (which I later learned was a mere twenty minutes)-and Mrs. Wheeler would slip me a peppermint candy to suck on which was her way of saying to be quiet. So, I started off concentrating on what the preacher's message was about and gradually drifted to thinking about what was for dinner, what books I could read that day and my plans for the week. In the South, dinner is actually "lunch," and the last meal of the day is "supper." When preaching was over, we would start to sing, "Praise God from whom all blessings flow, praise him for creatures here below, praise him above all heavenly hosts, praise Father, Son and Holy Ghost." That's the doxicology. Now, one time, Mrs. Wheeler visited the Holy Land and came back to tell me all about it. Her happiness was evident, and she expressed her readiness to meet the Lord.

Not long after that, she did just that. I could just see her now, waving and smiling at me from the Pearly Gates-it was a heartwarming sight.

In weekday school, I went by the nickname "Missy." (Apparently Michelle was too hard for kindergarten spelling) Weekday school was fun but afterwards we had to walk across the sidewalk with the teacher to nursery school to spend time with the baby kids. The owner of the nursery was named "Bill" and she, yes, she, was a "stem winder" as Mama Kate would say. I never could figure out how a woman could have the name "Bill" and I kept asking Nancy Kate if she was sure. (because she did like to fib) She assured me several times that it was. Anyway, Bill was nice most of the time and would take me on trips and we visited her pretty house. But, at some point, and for some reason, I started biting the baby kids. Not only did I make them cry but I would not stop. So, one day, Bill took my tiny hand and bit it as hard as she could. I didn't cry but it hurt. I just stared at her and pretended to be fine. Somehow, I knew if I cried, she would be the winner and if she wanted to play a game, I was going to win. I could not believe it and I told Nancy Kate. Bill said it was the only way to get me to stop and she was right because I didn't bite again. A week later Bill died, and Nancy Kate had to find a new nursery school. She found Plaza Baptist Church nursery so now I had two churches to go to and that's a whole lot of preaching. Little did I know how much I would need it.

Obviously, my anger started at an early age as I questioned life. Why did Michael and I have to go to the city with Nancy Kate? Why couldn't we be with my brothers? Why didn't my dad want to see me? Why was everything a secret? I missed my brothers, and I wanted us all to live together. Robin was the oldest and an extremely sweet and protective brother. Kerry was next and was always in trouble-like me. Kevin was closest to my age and had a penchant for teasing, but I did like his funny laugh. I tried to mock him as much as possible. Michael-the youngest-was a vision of innocence. His big blue eyes, blond hair, rosy cheeks, and ruby red lips painted a portrait of pure sweetness. In a world of confusion, Michael remained an angelic presence. As the years unfolded, each puzzle piece revealed a fragment of the truth. In quiet moments, I glimpsed the secret passages of my heart where memories and imagination gathered and I began to create my own unique world.

Either by blood or marriage, I was related to about everyone in Anson County. Ya see, Mama Kate was a Martin with eleven brothers and sisters. My mom married a Martin, but it was a separate set of Martins. There were about four sets. Mama Kate married Paul Alexander-hence the relation to Hezekiah Alexander of Charlotte. Mama Kate still lived in the big, white two-story house her dad built and she grew up in. I guess she got the house because she was the smartest. After her husband, Paul passed away, she used the house for boarding rooms. It had a tin roof and when it rained, the sound was heavenly. The front porch was covered and had a big swing. With its creaky floors, secret passages and ancestral portraits, the mysteries within those walls created a rich tapestry of memories. The second floor was used for storage which meant boxes and boxes of fun things to play with. There were books, toys, things I wasn't sure about and Knick knacks which Mama Kate said were pretty things to look at. That reminds me of a song we used to sing, "*knick knack paddy whack, give a dog a bone, this old man came rolling home.*" Singing was another part of our daily routine and at night I dreamed that this house was a portal to another dimension. I had quite an imagination. That's what Mama Kate always said.

Sometimes Nancy Kate would leave me and Michael there for a long time and I wasn't sure she was coming back so I would cry. I had to stop though because I did not want to hurt Mama Kate's feelings. Crying was for babies, and I pretended to be happy. My brothers did not like crying, especially Kerry. He would say, "I know you better not be crying." I would say, "no" and wipe my face and nose. As the days went by, I would start to feel better, and I established a routine that revolved around watching Mama Kate's TV show at 12:00 pm every day. It was called "As the World Turns." She had a tiny black and white tv that got one channel. As we watched her show, she would explain to me about all the characters and the rough life they were living. Every day I could not wait to see what happened next. After her show, she would send me outside to find pecans and that was great fun. I loved looking for pecans, but I hated shelling them. We also had to cut the ends off green beans. She cooked them with fat back and it was worth the work. While she cooked, I would head upstairs to go through boxes and play make believe games. When I finished, she would have supper ready. Mama Kate made the best chicken n dumplings, fried chicken, okra, blackberry cobbler, pecan pie and banana pudding. Well, that is enough to make you happy right there. Eventually Nancy Kate would come back for us, and we would go back to the city. She had a bright orange GTO which was embarrassing to me, but guys liked it for some reason. I learned those shiny metal holders with straps were called seat belts, but I wasn't sure what they were for. At home, I played house outside and picked berries for food while sweeping the dirt with a tree branch pretending it was a broom. In the sun-kissed haven of our front yard, my imagination was a painted canvas. The earth beneath my bare feet felt real but the rustling leaves whispered tales of make believe. When fireflies lit up the night like celestial lanterns, we would chase them with glass jars to capture their brilliance.

I loved animals and especially cats. My first cat was named Peppermint. She was all white with a pink nose. She would follow me around and I would talk to her. She was my best friend but that didn't last long. One day Nancy Kate took Peppermint away because she was going to have babies and we could not afford babies. We dropped her off in a neighborhood and she told me Peppermint would find a great family. I cried because I thought I was her great family. From that day forward, a little piece of my heart started to hurt. It would hurt increasingly over time. We got more than one channel on our black and white TV. TV's had "rabbit ears" to get the best reception, which was not great-but at the time, we didn't know any better. On TV I saw where a man had people kill a beautiful woman and she was going to have a baby. She was killed along with her friends for no reason. Then a doctor in the Army killed his two little girls and pregnant wife. People were marching in the streets with signs and screaming curse words. The police were hitting people with sticks, and everyone talked about a war. A war was a place where people just killed each other. They were all mad. At church we prayed and prayed about all the terrible things, but they never went away. I wondered what the use of praying was. Nancy Kate said she would have to ask the preacher about that, but I don't remember getting a response.

As long as I can remember a man named George would visit us. He was from Albemarle which was near Ansonville. George was nice in the daytime and turned into a monster at night. I would hear him and Nancy Kate fighting in her bedroom behind a closed door. Things would break and I could hear him punching the walls like a wild animal. I knew he was hitting her because she would scream out and cry. I would take Michael from his crib and hide in the closet. It became our sanctuary, our refuge from the chaos of the outside world. Michael was a good baby, and he would usually sleep through it. Every single time I wasn't sure whether Nancy Kate would make it through the night. I did not know what to do and had nowhere to go. At least if he came out, Michael and I might be hidden in the closet. I would think about ways to get away from him and run with Michael. This happened night after night, and I really wanted George to go away and never come back. When I would see the light come through the closet's slit doors, the house would be quiet. I would feed Michael his bottle, change his diaper and put him back in his crib. Then I would crawl into bed and pretend to be asleep. I would hear Nancy Kate getting up, so I knew she was alive. She never said a word about it, it was our pact of survival. I never got any sleep. On the nights that George didn't visit, I would stare at the ceiling and try to figure things out.

Then came the night when the church intervened. We packed our bags, whispered our prayers, and went to a hotel to hide. After a few days we went home, and I never saw George again. When George vanished, a newfound strength rose up within me. It seems in life, when you fix one problem, you just get another one. I had no time to celebrate. Whatever childhood I had would soon be gone forever. I got a new fluffy orange cat and named him "Tiger." I got to keep him because he wouldn't have babies. He would snuggle with me while I read books. Animals were my companions and words were my solace.

Nancy Kate started going out on the weekends and she would leave Michael and I with Tony. Tony was a neighbor who was almost grown up. When Nancy Kate left, Tony would have all his friends come over for a party. Tony put Michael to bed, and I was allowed to stay up for the party. I got to do all grown up things and felt important. Tony always said I would have to keep everything we did a secret, and I knew all about that. Boys and girls from high school were at this party and we played a game called "Spin the Bottle" where someone spins the bottle and if the bottle points to a boy and a girl, they must kiss. I already knew how to kiss because Tony showed me. Then we would drink strong tasting drinks which I later learned was alcohol. These drinks were nasty but made people laugh a lot. Sometimes we would play "the fainting game." This is when someone holds their breath, and another person comes up behind them and grabs them a certain way-this would make them faint. Kids still play this game today and of course; it is dangerous. We told ghost stories and played phone pranks. I had a Donny Osmond album which I played repeatedly. They would play that and the radio. They would smoke cigarettes and talk about the war. As I listened, I learned quite a bit about what was going on. There were people called Hippies that were going to take over the world and make peace. This sounded like such a great idea. They wore bell bottoms, listened to crazy music, and hugged all the time. Hippies liked to take drugs and listen to music. After a while, the parties stopped, and I was just always alone with Tony. Tony was a child molester. When terrible things happen, you can block them out and the memories are fuzzy. Some parts of my life are just blank, and this was one of them. When I started big school, I was nervous but there was no reason to be. I loved school more than anything. My first-grade teacher was named Mrs. Daniels. She had long blond hair and a pretty face. She talked softly and was an incredibly good teacher. We said the "Pledge of Allegiance" every day and had nap time on mats after lunch. There were kids my age to play with and a whole library full of books. My mom would take me to the big city library some weekends and I could check out as many books as I could carry. I read one after the other non-stop.

Sometimes we would go visiting. We went to my Aunt Mary's house across town. Aunt Mary was Mama Kate's sister. When we first moved to

Charlotte from Ansonville we lived in a duplex across the street from her. Aunt Mary had two grown sons, Uncle Johnny, and Uncle David. Uncle Johnny was very smart and handsome, but he never got married. He died early from brain cancer. Uncle David had a beautiful family, his wife, Nancy and his kids, Little David, Dale, and Kim. Sometimes we visited Mr. and Mrs. Hartis. They were the sweetest couple I had ever seen. It felt safe to be around them because you could just feel their love. They later went to a nursing home together and had rooms beside each other.

In the summertime I would stay with Mama Kate in Ansonville. I knew Mama Kate was very smart and I wanted to be like her when I grew up. She usually wore a long white nightgown and had thick, dark long hair that went down her back. She would braid it and taught me how to braid. She also taught me how to do needlepoint, but I never could figure out knitting. When Nancy Kate drove us to Ansonville she would go fast up and down the hills to make our stomachs flutter and then she would swerve the car from left to right and say it was a tornado. She talked about what it was like to be the only child growing up with her parents. Nancy Kate said that Mama Kate once had a hat shop down the road and always wore pretty hats. Years ago, she said everyone wore hats and in England they still do. The Mayor of Ansonville was Joe Estridge and he lived down by the railroad tracks-where I never once saw a train but always heard it come at night. In town there were two stores across from each other and one was owned by Bill Hildreth, the meanest man in town. My dad owned a store in town and usually rented it out. It closed after my grandfather, Jesse Waddell or "Bop" died. There was a post office, bank, churches, and a big scary looking house with an iron gate around it. Later Sonny Beachum bought this house, tore it down and made a classic car museum. Nancy Kate once dated Sonny Beachum, but Mama Kate said he didn't finish high school and would never amount to a hill of beans. She was wrong. He became a millionaire. Down the lane, was the house where Bop and Mama Mammy lived. Across the street from their house was the little white house where me and my mom, dad and brothers lived before my family split. Next to the little white house was Ansonville Elementary School and then the baseball field. The Fire Station was across the street. Once a year, there was Barbeque at the Fire Station and a parade on Main Street. Most of the kids there had nicknames like "Little Man," "Butter Bean," "Queen Bee," and "Scooter." There was a church on every street. Mama Kate went to the Ansonville Baptist Church but most of my kin went to Red Hill Baptist Church and that's where all my family was buried. I was related to most people in town and cousins were like pecans at Mama Kate's-just scattered everywhere. Around the corner from the fire station was my Aunt Eliza's house, which was Mama Kate's sister. I always wondered why everyone called her Aunt Eliza. She wasn't everyone's Aunt. As I grew up, I realized they were saying Ann Eliza. Ann Eliza's grandkids were "Big Ed" and Iris. I would visit them along with all my other cousins. Down from Aunt Eliza's was Tootie Edward's house and she had peacocks which I found fascinating. They were beautiful. They wandered around in the backyard and opened their fan of purple and blue feathers. Each feather had an eye dot. Mama Kate said I could never be proud like the peacocks because it was a sin, but it was okay for them to shine because they were just showing God's glory. Next to Mama Kate's house was Aunt Connie and Uncle Fincher. Mama Kate lived in "the Martin Homestead" which sat proudly on the hill. It had a huge porch and swing. I used to swing and look down the hill at the Brown's property for entertainment. They lived in a tiny brown house about the size of Mama Kate's kitchen. I never saw the parents, but barefooted kids were always going in and out. The sound of the screen door slamming, and their mama yelling was non-stop. I tried to count them, but they would not stay still. There must have been ten of them so how did they all fit in there? Where did they all sleep and how did the mama feed all those kids? They didn't have grass in their yard, just red dirt. Sometimes the little ones would go to the road, and I would get frantic. The kids always played in the dirt and were brown, which is probably where they got their name. They never noticed me on the hill watching them. One Sunday they "borrowed" Miss Tootie's lawn mower and drove it to church. About three of them at a time would ride back and forth. Once when I was grown, I was driving one Sunday in Ansonville, and I saw three people riding down the street on a riding lawnmower. To most people that would seem strange, but I just thought to myself, "hey it's the Browns' going to church."

When school started back, I went to second-grade and my teacher was Miss Waldrop. She looked like the granny from the Beverly Hillbillies but was not that feisty and did not carry a shotgun. I remember around this time; I started making friends. One of my friends was Sandy Nealy from down the street. We played hopscotch, jacks and jumped rope. Sometimes we could even have sleepovers. Another friend was Daphne Stephens. She lived in the projects with her mom so I could not spend the night there. Later Daphne's mom married a nice man and they moved to a big pretty house in the country, and she got her very own horse. Before I knew it, the school year was over, and it was time to go back to Ansonville. I love going to Mama Kate's now because I got a new bicycle, and it was at her house. My brothers came by and taught me how to ride it.

One day I asked Mama Kate to tell me stories about the old days and she did. In Ansonville there is a mansion in town that was built for General William Alexander Smith and his family. The plantation was beautiful and there was a pond, pasture, cabins, and Oak trees all around. Everyone called it General Smith's house even though he was no longer alive. My grandmother and her family used to live in a house next door before "the Martin Homestead" was built. The house they lived in was haunted and a ghost would come down the stairs every morning at 6 am. All the Martin family agreed. It was the ghost of a woman that had fell to her death there one morning. I later visited this house, and it was exactly the way she described it. I visited the mansion too over the years and hoped someone would take care of it and not let it fall in. General Smith was a very prominent man and a fixture in the Civil War. He owned businesses, started a church, and built the first Female College. Although he was intelligent and successful, his personal life was tragic. He was injured during the war and suffered a permanent limp. He had three children that died at an early age. Etta was born, Nona was born and there was a boy that was not named because he only lived two days. Nona died when she was six years old from Typhoid Fever. All the women at the college got it and started to die. Then the college was burned to the ground. When Etta was nineteen, she died of pneumonia. According to Mama Kate, the General had her pickled and left her in her room for a year with nothing changed or disturbed since the day she died. She was in a glass case and people came from all around to visit her and say goodbye. She was later buried in Eastview Cemetery. I wasn't sure how a person could be "pickled," but I knew Mama Kate did not lie. Near General Smith's plantation was Gaddy's Goose Pond and people came from all over the world to feed the geese. It later became the Pee Dee National Wildlife Refuge.

Mama Kate said that her mother was called Nannie Martin, and her father was Jefferson Martin. They had twelve children, about half girls and half boys. Nannie died working in the garden when she was in her forties. Mama Kate said it was from having too many kids. That wears your body out. That's when she told me how children were born after the mom and dad would decide one day, they just wanted one. The Mama's stomach would grow and one day a baby would come out. Mama Kate had a baby girl after my mom was born but she was born dead which was called "stillborn." She said babies died back then because no one went to the hospital, they had their babies at home, and they did not know what they were doing. All of Mama Kate's brothers and sisters would grow up to have big happy families except for Brent and Julian. I always got these two mixed up. They both died young. Julian was kicked in the head by a mule and Brent was robbed and murdered on the railroad track in Norwood. I was fascinated by all the stories Mama Kate would tell so I thought this might be a suitable time to find out about all the secrets and, lo and behold, I was right. Mama Kate answered my questions like it was nothing. If I had asked Nancy Kate, she would have lied or ignored me. They were nothing alike. I asked Mama Kate about my dad. She said he was a cowboy and a very mean man who beat Nancy Kate. I did not necessarily believe that because I knew this would be Nancy Kate's side of the story. Mama Kate said my dad "Buddy" had lots of women on the side. Then I asked Mama Kate about George. I knew for sure he would beat Mama, so I was curious about the answer. It was not the answer I expected. She said, "Well, let me just tell you the whole story." George was the principal at Robin, Kerry and Kevin's school and Nancy Kate was his secretary. Mama Kate kept me while the boys went to school and Nancy Kate went to work at their school. Then Nancy Kate started seeing George and George was Michael's daddy. Well hellfire and brimstone, no wonder my dad was so mean. She said there was a big scandal and Nancy Kate had to leave town. My dad had lots of land and money, and my mom traded me for her part of the land and money. I asked her why my dad never wanted to see me, and she said he married a woman named Ann Phillips. Ann had three boys and a girl so now they had a new family which included my brothers but not me. My dad had built a new fancy house for her, and she did not want me or mom around ever. I felt sick to my stomach.

Mama Kate was telling me it was time for my bath, and I could hear the rain starting to fall on the tin roof. I told her I did not want to take a bath so she said I could just take a "whore's bath" which was splashing water on yourself. Sometimes she called it a "bird's bath." I knew what a whore was because Mama Kate told me that too. A whore was like all the women that slept with my dad. Later that week Nancy Kate picked me up and said she had a surprise for me. I was going to YMCA camp for a week. YMCA camp was the most fun ever. We played dodge ball, steal the flag, basketball and made arts and crafts. When it was time for swimming lessons, something bad happened. A man was my swim teacher and he kept touching me. I had a bad feeling about him. At first, I thought it was my imagination but then I was walking by the man's locker room to get to the pool, and he called my name. I walked into the locker room, and he was standing there with no clothes on and a strange look on his face. This reminded me of bad things. After that I was glad camp only lasted a week, but I didn't get to learn freestyle because when it was time for swim class, I would hide. It seemed like whenever something good happened, then something bad would happen. When I got home, I looked at myself in the mirror. My face was a perfect oval shape, my hair was long, and silky-it was chestnut colored with blonde streaks from the sun and my eyes were bright blue. I really had every reason to like myself but instead I felt empty inside.

CHAPTER 2 SEEKING JUSTICE

I didn't know what depression was. It felt like I was in a dark lonely hole, and I couldn't escape. The world seemed so cold and evil. Attempts at bringing light into the world felt futile. I tried to concentrate on the things in life that made me happy. In fact, I had a little notebook in the shape of a heart. Each page said Happiness is....and I would write things that made me happy. Happiness is "getting an ice cream sandwich at lunch." Happiness is "making new friends." Happiness is "wearing my favorite blue socks." Sometimes it's just the little things. My third-grade teacher was Mrs. Bivens. Before school, my mom would drop me off at Plaza Road Baptist Church Nursery and I would watch Sesame Street while I waited for Sandra. Sandra Wellman was my best friend. We would gather our books and walk hand in hand to school every day. We were always in the same classes. Sandra had pretty tanned skin, white teeth, and thick long hair. Her little brother Jimmy was Michael's age and they played together. After school we walked hand in hand back to nursery. Plaza Baptist looked more like a school than a church. It was a small rectangular brick building but the playground in the back was huge. My favorite part of the playground was the sandbox. One day I was running and fell flat onto the wooden sides of the sandbox. I had my breath knocked out of me and I thought I was dying. As I looked around no one noticed, and everything was happening in slow motion. It brought back a hidden memory. I was in the ocean underwater, and I couldn't hold my breath any longer. I looked up to the top of the water as I sank deeper and deeper, and fear set in. Fear was my greatest enemy. In an instant someone jerked me up out of the water and I started to hear voices. As I looked around, I was back in the playground. I walked over to the teacher and told her what happened. She said, " Oh you'll be fine. You just got the wind knocked out of ya Missy." It was time to go in and I looked around for Sandra. When I found her, she looked me in the eyes, and it was as if she could read my mind. She grabbed my hand and gave me a reassuring smile.

When it rained and we couldn't go outside, we did other fun things like making colored potato chips, arts, crafts, and coloring. Then we got our mats and blankets out of our cubbies for naptime. I hated naptime and so did Sandra. We felt it was our duty to try and keep everyone awake, much to the discernment of our teachers. One of us usually ended up standing in the corner for a while. After naptime, there were snacks and story time. One teacher took story time to a whole new level. She told us true crime stories. There was a man with a hook instead of a hand that opened car doors when lovers were parking, and he would kill them with his hook. There were people that worshipped the devil at a place called "The Devil's Tramping Ground." The world was coming to an end soon and there was a place in the ocean called "The Bermuda Triangle" where boats and planes disappeared off the earth. She told ghost stories about " Sally's Bridge" and there was a ghost that hitchhiked because she never made it home alive. At night I would go over these stories in my mind. That's when fear would grip me, set in, and take over. I just closed my eyes and waited for someone to pull me up out of that ocean of fear.

When fourth grade started our teacher was Mrs. Logan. She was the best teacher yet. We had a new girl named "Sally." She was skinny, wore dirty clothes and had greasy hair cut into a bowl cut. All the kids made fun of her. She was very pale and appeared to be sick. I began to feel deeply sorry for her. She was always alone and sad. Sandra and I were always the leaders and had fun, so I decided to be her friend. She talked very softly and was smart. The first time I saw her smile, my heart almost skipped a beat. It was a beautiful thing. I treated her like my equal because-she was. I enjoyed talking to her and getting to know her. She had just moved here from out of the state and lived with her mother and they were extremely poor. We were poor too. I always got the free lunch ticket but, they were worse off than me. Sometimes she didn't get to eat supper, so I would give her some of my food. She ate like she was starving. As I got to know her, the other kids did too and accepted her. She seemed genuinely happy and started to come out of her shell. One day in the bathroom she said she had something to show me, but I couldn't tell anyone. I agreed. She turned and pulled up her shirt and it looked like there was a burn on her back in the shape of an iron. It was horrible. I asked her how that happened and told her to go to the school nurse, but she said she couldn't because her mama did that. If she ever told on her mama, she would really get a worse beating. I thought to myself, "what could be worse than this?" I let her talk and listened but the more she did, the more furious I became. I could not keep this secret. She needed help and showing me was a cry for help. So, when I was alone with Mrs. Logan, I told her. She listened intently and told me not to worry. She would take care of it. It made me feel so relieved that Sally would be saved. I hoped the police would rescue her and put her mother in jail.

The next day, Sally wasn't in her seat, and I started to worry. Before class started Mrs. Logan made an announcement that Sally would not be back.

She had moved away. My heart sank. I couldn't wait until recess to ask Mrs. Logan what happened. And when I did, I couldn't believe the answer. A Social Worker went to her house yesterday and this morning, Sally's mom called and took her out of school. I was incredulous. I said, "Mrs. Logan, we have to do something" but I could tell from the sad look in her eyes, there was no use. She was just silent. I trusted her and Sally trusted me. Mrs. Logan told me she was sorry. Tears welled up in my eyes and I walked away so she didn't see them. I was mad. All I could do was pray. I prayed for Sally, and I prayed for God to get me away from Tony. Everyone was put on this earth with a purpose. My purpose was to seek justice and my very first attempt had failed miserably. Or did it? This scared Sally's mother, and she would stop beating her. This would give Sally the courage to stand up to her mother. I would never know.

That winter I got extremely sick and had to go to the hospital. I had pneumonia. The doctors gave me penicillin, but I got worse every day. The more they gave me, the worse I got. Not only could I not breathe but I started having severe stomach cramps, swelling, hives and I was miserable. I thought doctors knew everything, but I heard them say that they didn't understand what was happening to me. I had pneumonia but the medicine was not helping. One day my mom brought in a bag from Mrs. Logan, and it was filled with cards that the kids at school made for me. I had balloons and flowers. Now I can read these cards over and over. I loved them and worried about all the work I was missing. How would I ever get caught up now? I prayed to get better and one day a doctor said they were changing me to a new antibiotic. I had read about antibiotics at school. They were medicines to fight bacterial infections. The next day the swelling and hives went down. My stomach stopped cramping. After a few days, I started to breathe without making a wheezing noise. A week later, I could breathe without oxygen. The doctors said I could go home in a few days and that I was allergic to penicillin. They told me to never take it again. My mom wrote that down and mumbled something about my dad being allergic to it also. When I did return to school, everyone was so happy to see me. Mrs. Logan let me take work home at night to get caught up. I made straight A's just like always.

One day Nancy Kate got a letter from Buddy Martin's mom-Virigina. She requested that I spend some time with her and her husband that summer. I was so excited. I would get to meet my dad and we would spend time together now. It was all I could think about. They lived in Ansonville on Martin Road. As we drove down Martin Road, I saw cow pastures on both sides of the road, a baseball field, a fire tower and an exceptionally long brick house with a circular driveway and little buildings all around it. There was a gas pump, and cars were everywhere. A sign said, "Martin's

Used Cars." A tall gray-haired woman in a housecoat with snaps came to the side door under the carport with two huge dogs that looked like teddy bears. She said to call her "Mama Gina." She introduced one of her dogs to me like he was human. She said, " this is Baby Dog, and he is a Chow, Missy." There were other Chows that were walking by as they came single file in a line from the house, but you could tell "Baby Dog" was special. Then it occurred to me that I had never met anyone that loved animals like I did. She went on fussing about them, and I started to pet them. Nancy Kate made a quick exit and Mama Gina showed me how to take care of the dogs. Each one had their own bowl and got a scoop of dog food with a little oil poured on top. That would make their coat shiny. We brushed them and talked as if we had always known each other. She took me to a spacious room with books and puzzles all around. I couldn't believe it. I was in heaven. So, we read and did puzzles while waiting for her husband, "Daddy Jim" to come home and take us out to eat. Mama Gina didn't like to cook, and we only went to restaurants. Daddy Jim was dark skinned and had slicked back black hair. He was incredibly good looking and so sweet to me. Mama Gina and Daddy Jim were quite different. Mama Gina chain smoked cigarettes and drank coke all day. Daddy Jim didn't but he never complained about the smoke. As I would learn later, Mama Gina drove fast, and Daddy Jim drove very slowly. Mama Gina would stay up late and sleep in. Daddy Jim went to bed early and was gone before we ever got up. I found out later, he got up every day at 5 a.m. and went to breakfast. That's why they slept in different beds. I slept in a pull-out bed in front of the TV and their TV had colored pictures. I had never seen such a thing. Me and Mama Gina watched game shows like "The Price is Right" and "Wheel of Fortune." I couldn't believe how much we had in common, but she was not like anyone I had ever met. She was fierce. She could be mean and even said the "N" word. The first time I heard it, I thought I heard her wrong. And then she said it repeatedly. I kept quiet because I knew she must have grown up this way and didn't know any better. One day, Daddy Jim asked me if I wanted to go with him instead of staying home with Mama Gina. I agreed and he went to breakfast and came back to get me later. Me and Mama Gina didn't "do" 5 am. Daddy Jim and I drove around and looked at cars to buy, stopped at Fred Randall's store and got cokes and hoop cheese, and then stopped at various places to talk to people and collect money. I had never seen so much money as Daddy Jim had in his wallet. After a late lunch we headed home. This made me think, instead of being an archeologist, I should sell cars. What a fantastic job he had. He used to work for the Department of Transportation and worked on roads. He said, "When the roads sparkle Missy, I built them." He went into long detail about why the roads would sparkle but whenever people talked about technical things, it sounded to me like, "blah, blah, blah, blah, blah." I pretended to listen intently because I loved to hear his voice. He reminded me of an older Elvis Presley. Later that week, he told me he had a surprise for me. He took me to the barn and there in the middle of the barn was the most beautiful thing I had ever seen-a pony. I spent a great deal of time in the barn after that. I would also go up the abandoned fire tower. Mama Gina told me I could. Some of the steps were missing and when you got to the top there was a trap door that you opened, and you could go inside. I could see all of Ansonville, even Mama Kate's house. The wind blew hard, and the steel made a creaking noise. I would go up there and read a book, take a break, and look all around. I thought to myself, this must be what heaven feels like and I did not want to go home. I wanted to stay here forever. I started to think about Mama Kate and hoped she wouldn't be sad now because I had another grandmother. Mama Kate's husband had died a long time ago and I had never had a grandfather. When I got down from the fire tower, I asked Mama Gina if I could stay with them longer than two weeks, and she said she would call my mom. I ended up spending the whole summer. She told my mom I needed to spend time with my new pony that I named "Shorty."

So, I stayed and began my routine with Mama Gina. After staying up late to watch TV, we would wake up around 11 am and she would bring me a big Styrofoam cup with coke and ice in it. She would say, "here's your breakfast Missy." I thought that she was the coolest person ever. She would start smoking and we would go around feeding all the dogs and I would go visit and feed Shorty. Sometimes Mama Gina would take me to see her mom, Mama Mammie in the nursing home. It smelled like pee. The first time we went, a nurse stopped her at the door. "Miss Virigina, Miss Virginia, your mama is in trouble again." Mama Mammie was a hundred years old and was "SEAnile" which meant she didn't remember things anymore. The nurse went on to say Mama Mammie had snuck into people's rooms and woke them up and even escaped out the backdoor in her wheelchair one day. This nurse must not have known Mama Gina very well. Mama Gina's face turned red, and she said, "Well what the hell am I paying you bunch of idiots for? Do I have to come down here and hold your hand? Why are you telling ME that YOU can't do your job?" Before she could continue another nurse rushed up to save her. She said, "I'm so sorry Miss Virigina, this won't ever happen again. We will take care of everything." Mama Gina said, "Well see that you do." Then she slung her big pocketbook around and almost hit that nurse. She said, "Come on Missy." When I first met Mama Mammie, I was surprised. She was just as happy as she could be. She thought I was Aunt Mills, who was my dad's sister. She told stories about all the rabbits that would come to visit her. She said they hid in her drawers at night. Mama Gina said in a stern loud voice, "Now Mama, did you try to sneak out again?" Mama Mammie said the nurses threw her out and it was cold out there. (Since it was 85 degrees every day, I don't think she froze) We brought her some food, and she ate like Daddy Jim and me. (lots of food and real fast) Mama Gina said, "Nobody's gonna take it away from you Mama." Then it hit me. Mama Gina reminded me of Eunice's mama on "The Carol Burnett Show." She even looked like her. It was hilarious.

That night Mama Gina cooked dinner and it was so good. I said, "Mama Gina you are a great cook." She said, "Well I know that Missy, I said I don't like to cook. I didn't say I didn't know how." She showed me how to wash dishes using scalding hot water. We made cookies and when we finished, I got to lick the bowl, the spoon and the beaters that came out of the mixer. She said, "now isn't cooking fun?" sarcastically. And I said not really but eating is. "She said, that's right." She lit a cigarette while I poured out our cokes. Then we went in to watch our shows. On some days, people would come over to play with me-mostly my stepbrother, Eric. He was my dad's new wife's son. We had a fun time together. He was nice for a boy. But whenever my brother Kevin came with him, it was a disaster. We fought non-stop. Mama Gina had made me a shirt with 7 up cans on it. It was ugly but I had to wear it to make her happy. Kevin said, "Where did you get that shirt? You never wear cool stuff." I said, "shut up Mama Gina made this, and she is going to be mad if I don't wear it." He just laughed and would not let it go. When it was time to go out to eat, he said, "I'm not going with her looking like that. She's embarrassing." That was it. I punched him and he said, "Mama Gina, she hit me." Of course, we stopped after Mama Gina threatened to take us both out back and beat us with a hickory stick. Eric usually came alone.

Then one day Mama Gina said, "Your dad is coming for lunch." I could not believe it. I would finally get to see my dad and we could spend time together. He would love me just like Daddy Jim. I couldn't wait. Mama Gina started to fix him a sandwich and I sat watching the door in anticipation. Right on time, the most handsome man I had ever seen walked in. He had on a western shirt, cowboy hat, boots, and jeans. He looked like a movie star. It was as if I wasn't even in the room. He completely ignored me, and I was in shock. He ate his sandwich, talked to Mama Gina, and left without saying a word to me. I thought Mama Gina would explain when he left, but she didn't seem to even notice anything was wrong. Mama Kate had been right. He was a mean man and for some reason, he didn't want to have anything to do with me. This made me sad. I had made a bargain with God. If he would bring me a dad, I would be good from now on. This isn't what I had in mind. But God has a strange way of answering prayers sometimes.

When Nancy Kate came to pick me up, I did not want to leave. She said she had some news to tell me. She was getting married to a man named "Richard" and he would be my stepdad. He was from the North, and we would be traveling up there to meet his parents and relatives. I had never been anywhere except Anson County and now I was going all the way to Boston, Massachusetts and through New York City. Richard's three children would be going with us. When I met Richard, I noticed what a nice man he was and how funny he talked. I could barely understand him. All his A's were long and drawn out like "park the car" was "PAAAArk the CAAAAr." I had never seen or heard of a northern person before. Mama Gina said, "they were all damn Yankees", so I figured I was in for a fight. I was wrong. The next few months were like a whirlwind. We traveled, sold the house, they got married and we bought a condominium to stay in until our new house was built. Yes, I was finally moving away. I was finally free. And you know how God is good. He answered my prayers in ways I could never imagine. Now I was moving away from the terrible things, and I had not just one dad but two. (even though one didn't acknowledge me) I was not only ready to take on this cruel world, but I was gonna kick ass.

CHAPTER 3 CANDY CRUSH

Well, I might have kicked some ass but there is no doubt I also got my ass kicked quite a bit. In fact, I was diagnosed with Post Traumatic Stress Disorder. Being strong is not when you never feel fear. Being strong is when you feel fear and move forward afraid. When I pull into the driveway and look up at this big beautiful antebellum mansion, I try to imagine what it was like when General Smith lived here. His original fifteen hundred acres is now down to twenty acres. Instead of white, the house is a light yellow with red rustic trim. There are decorative lights, balls, statues and the front and back are perfectly manicured. The Carriage House is now a three-car garage. The dairy is a shed. Behind the house in a semi-circle are three cottages. Two used to be slave houses and thank goodness, I got the one that used to be an outdoor kitchen because those slave houses have memories etched into the walls. Further back, the smokehouse and grain/icehouse are also cottages. Then there is the big red barn that is three stories high, a fenced pasture with a pond and dock and to the right lies the garden. Don added a pool, jacuzzi and koi pond directly behind the house. The entire estate has over a hundred oak trees. I tried to count them one day but gave up. On the side of the house is the garden shed, well, and rose garden.

Don is Dr. Donald R.H. Byrd Jr., and I am proud to call him a friend. He is an international ambassador, speaks eight different languages and his assets total millions of dollars. He didn't tell me that last part, but I always check everyone out. I guess it's second nature when you are a skip tracer. He doesn't act like it though. He is very down to earth and unassuming. We share a love of history, wine, animals and much more. We have our differences. He is a hard-core liberal Democrat, and I am a conservative Republican, but politics don't come between us. Now that I am fifty-five years old, I have become more of a spiritual being and I'm not exactly sure how this works, but I hear from God.

To you has been given the secret of the kingdom of God, but for those outside, everything comes in parables: in order that "they may indeed look, but not perceive, and may indeed listen, but not understand."

Mark 4:11-12

At the end of last year, I felt a calling to leave work, my live-in boyfriend, and Charlotte NC behind and move back to Ansonville NC. As January approached, I felt a sense of urgency. I had planned to move to one of the cottages earlier, but they weren't finished yet and time just slipped away. I made it here at the end of January and a little over a month later, the COVID-19 virus hit. I am considered "high risk" because I have severe asthma called "Eosinophilic Asthma."

When I pulled up next to the cottage, I opened the trunk to get the T-Tops out to put back on the Camero in case it rained. I remember the first time I ever saw a Camero. I think it was a blue 1968. I told Nancy Kate, or "Nana" as we call her now, that "when I grow up, that's the car I'm getting." She said, "Oh they won't make them anymore by the time you start driving Missy." Four Cameros later, I'm just shaking my head. The smell of muscadines and the rattle of the train at night remind me of my early childhood years spent in Ansonville with Mama Kate. Her big white house was still right down the street. I knew Mama Kate and all my other relatives were smiling down at me.

The main reason I chose this cottage was because of the air circulation. It had high "A" framed ceilings, a back room, and a staircase that led to a trap door and a loft. The trap door opened to a place where they used to store food. Now it was my bedroom, and my favorite part was the old circular window high on the wall. At night I slept facing the window and during the day, I would turn the other way and watch tv or look over the balcony below. "Alaya" the cat loved to jump from beam to beam like an acrobat. "Charlie" and "Casey," my chihuahuas, were happier than two peas in a pod. They had their routine, which involved running all over the plantation, returning for a treat, and following me around. "Koya" and "Leila," the two ferrets, are let out of their cage twice a day. Most of their time in the cage is spent sleeping in their hammock together. Outside of the cage, they are as mischievous as two little ferrets can be.

The main house looks different than it did when I was little. Don decorated it with expensive paintings, fixtures, carpets, and furniture that he got from his travels all over the world. My favorite room is the downstairs bedroom behind the staircase. It has built-in bookcases on every wall filled with books. Don wrote many of them, thirty-five to be exact. Not only was he a published author but he was a college professor up north at one point. When the power went out in the cottages, this is the room I chose to stay in. When you walk through the hall to the staircase, there are many rooms downstairs, but the front porch is the most impressive feature of this Southern mansion. It stretches across the entire front of the house and has two huge colonial style columns that stretch up towards the balcony. When you head upstairs, there is an inside slave bedroom at the top of the stairs. The female inside slave would lock all the doors at night and get up early in the morning to make breakfast. When you get to the top of the stairs, the bedroom on the right originally belonged to "Etta Smith"-the General's daughter. She lived from 1870-1888 and died from pneumonia. As I looked around the room, I searched for signs of her being "pickled and left there" like Mama Kate said but there was no trace of Etta Smith unless you count her "spirit presence." There were so many rumors about the Plantation over the years. It was hard to tell the truth from fiction, but Mama Kate was close to being correct. I think most people were preserved and kept at home for a while before their burial. They even spent time with them and took pictures with the body around that time, so it was possible. Etta had a sister named "Nona" that lived to be five years old and there was a baby boy that lived for a day. The next room would have been Nona's when she was alive. This bedroom had a little door that went to an attic space. The attic space led to the outside balcony where you could see all around the front of the property. It was a grand sight. Across the hall, the largest bedroom had belonged to Mr. and Mrs. Smith and the bedroom to the left would have been a guest bedroom. Each room had a fireplace for heat. Now each room also has a TV and bathroom that Don added. Don's bedroom is downstairs by the kitchen. The sunroom and parlor are by the library. He uses a golf cart to get around the grounds and has a housekeeper, groundskeeper, and caregiver. (Helena, Mario, and Marcio)

When I first moved in, Don came over to the cottage to visit me and my mom was there. She used to cook for him and they were friends. I showed him my diplomas for my master's degree and Bachelor of Science Degree. He said, "you know I have a FUD" and I said, "what's that?" He said a FUD was a PHD. I was impressed. Don, my mom and my dad were all eighty-three years old, and I worried about them. Don and my dad both had liver disease and suffered from rheumatic fever when they were children. My dad had permanent heart damage and Don had permanent nerve damage. Other than that, these two men were complete opposites. People say my dad is a hero, but Don is the real hero. And mom, well, she's just batshit crazy. To be more precise, she has a narcissistic personality disorder. Kerry says that's because she was the only child and spoiled rotten. She is starting to have seizures and I have tried to take care of her, but she is extremely hard to deal with. I learned to put up huge boundaries with her. I haven't talked to my dad in a year. He is terribly angry at me because I stole his toothbrush at Thanksgiving and sent it off with mine to a lab for a DNA test. It came back 99.99% that he IS the father. I thought that would make him act like one, but it didn't. He called me and screamed at me when he heard through the grapevine (Kerry) that his toothbrush was stolen. As soon I received the test paper results in the mail, I dropped everything and drove to Ansonville to show him. The look on his face was priceless. He later told Kerry to tell me that he never wanted to see me or my brother Robin again. (That's another saga) So I decided Don would be my new father figure. Don didn't have any children. His partner died many years ago and he had a picture of him on his bedroom wall alongside his own picture. They were both very handsome. I told Don he looked like Marlon Brando. His partner was from Greece and looked like Burt Reynolds. I knew they were soulmates and Don would never love again. There is a gold plaque outside with both of their names on it.

I thought a piece of paper would make you love me.

I thought a piece of paper would set me free

I thought a piece of paper would bring us closer

But it was never meant to be

I have lived all my life to please you....

Now my father in heaven will see me through

I wake up in the mornings when Charlie starts licking my ear. I open my eyes and Alaya is staring down at me. I feel a warm Casey-like lump on my hip. I know if I move, they will all scatter like Christmas morning. Alaya thinks that I don't see her, so she moves closer, and I feel her wet nose touch mine. As I stretch my legs, they all jump to attention and are preparing to dive towards the stairs. I let them all out and when they come back in, I let the ferrets out of their cage. I fill the ferret's dishes and Koya starts to gobble her food so she can go play with Charlie. Once I asked my daughter Brandi, "why do they love each other so much?" She said, "they are both mean asses and mean asses love each other." As I looked her in the eye, we both smiled. We were so much alike-except I am not bi-polar or gay. My older children, Devin and Chase lived far away, and I didn't like to think about it because I missed my grandchildren so much. When my friends talked about their grandchildren, I felt envious. Chase lives in Asheville NC and has a daughter named Josie. My daughter Devin lives in

Freeport, Florida and has three children-Terry, Lily, and Primrose. After the virus is over, I plan to see them all. Koya jumped out of the cage and attacked Charlie as he walked up. Leila wasn't as feisty as Koya, but she was sneaky. One morning I cleaned my coffee cup, poured coffee in it, and heated it for a minute because I like it extremely hot. I drank it throughout the morning refilling it a few times until I was finished. As I lay the cup in the sink and turned it sideways, three different earrings fell out. I just stared at them. How was that possible? They were NOT there previously so where did these earrings come from? I picked them up and took them to where I keep earrings that are missing one and sure enough their matches were there. Now I knew either a spirit did this or Leila did it and as I looked around for Leila, she was sneaking around like a thief so I'm quite sure it was her. Either way these earrings came from the floor, and I've been drinking some "dirty ass" coffee like it was Starbucks. After prayer and meditation, exercising, putting the ferrets up and checking the news, I like to play Candy Crush. Candy Crush is like life. Some levels are hard, some are super hard, and some are nightmarishly hard. In life, there isn't a warning like there is in Candy Crush. I'm on level 1102 and it feels about the same for my life. Sometimes when I play the game and the level is hard, I think, "I will never get through this level." I always do. Some days I go from level to level to level and think, "I will never lose." I do. Forest Gump said that "life was like a box of chocolates because you never know what you get." I don't believe so. I remember an index of flavors under the lid. To me, life is more like "Candy Crush." Each level is a surprise and a challenge. No one else can play YOUR game for YOU. If they did, it would be THEIR game. Just stay calm, play your game and you will make it to the next level. Sometimes it's quick and painless. Sometimes it takes a little patience.

CHAPTER 4 CANDLEWOOD

My new stepdad's name was Richard Crovi. That is a Northern Italian name. After the big wedding at Plaza Presbyterian Church, we went to Bridgewater, Massachusetts to visit his parents and then St. Paul, Minnesota to visit his sister, Irene. Even though it was summer, it was cold in Massachusetts. We took a ferry to Martha's Vineyard and Cape Cod. His family was genuinely nice, and they didn't seem to be "damn Yankees" at all. They all talked very funny, and I tried not to stare at them, but they were like aliens on a spaceship. They had the greatest Italian food ever and even talked in Italian sometimes. His mama would say "mangiare mangiare" which meant "eat, eat." To me it sounded like "monja monja." Baseball was a big deal there and everyone went to play when they got off work. Large happy extended families were what I remember most.

The only thing I remember about Minnesota is the gigantic mosquitoes. If you're from Minnesota, I apologize but, in my defense, Prince wasn't famous yet and Paisley Park wasn't even thought of. So "shout out" to the Twin Cities and the home of Prince Rogers Nelson. When we came home, all our belongings were already moved to the new condominium. The condominiums were called "Candlewood" and we lived on "Old Lantern Way." This was the perfect place for kids my age. Candlewood was inside a huge brick wall. Every unit had kids. We had a clubhouse, pool, basketball court and woods on the side to build a fort. I spent most of my time outside with my new best friends, Mary Beth, and Darlene. I think their parents were from the North because they went to Catholic school. The rest of us were bused across town to Lincoln Heights which was the ghetto. Black people were bused to the white side of town and white people were bused to the black side of town. This was to make everyone get along better. I never realized that we were not getting along except for things I saw on TV and read about in History class.

In Ansonville, everyone talked about the Civil War like it just happened. I never even noticed people's skin color and all the Yankees I had met seemed genuinely nice. To me, people were equal and that meant boys and girls too. When I play basketball with the neighborhood boys, I am incredibly good and make almost every shot. I play every day, and no one can play as good as I do. All the boys know it. Everything was great until a new kid moved in. He came to play and asked why a girl was playing. After I beat his ass in basketball, the other boys laughed at him, and he asked me my name. I said "Michelle." He said, "Well let's give Michelle a pink belly!" The next thing I knew they all grabbed me, and I went down on the ground. They pulled up my shirt and started slapping my stomach and tickling me. I HATED being tickled and prayed I did not wet my pants. I started fighting back like a Hellcat. Boys started to scatter except the new boy. I grabbed his shirt and must have scratched his eyes out because they started bleeding. I never saw an eyeball bleed. I brushed off my T shirt and jeans and he was holding his face. I said, "you better get that checked out Mama's boy." When I went home my knees were bleeding through my jeans. What just happened? The doorbell rang and I could hear a lady screaming that my mama was going to pay her son's doctor's bills. Of course, Nancy Kate didn't take up for me even though they started it, and my belly was bright red. Richard was still at work, but he would have taken up for me. Richard was the sweetest man I had ever met, and he really had his hands full with me. His kids were mild mannered and smart. He told Nancy Kate that I was just a "tomboy", and I would grow out of it. After that I took a break from basketball and hung out with my friend, Stephanie Smith. We went swimming every day and her dad helped us build a fort in the woods. He didn't know we were building it to go smoke cigarettes. Stephanie got them from her mama, and they were called "Eve" cigarettes. This was the summer of my life- even when I fell out of a car and chipped my front tooth. The dentist just bonded it back together. Richard asked me nicely not to jump on his car while he was driving it. I loved Richard and felt sorry for him because he was stuck with me and Nancy Kate. Michael was a good kid most of the time. He stayed out of trouble. Eckerd Drug store closed their central office and Nancy Kate got a job selling advertising. Since she worked on straight commission, this started a constant money struggle for her because it was either feast or famine. She couldn't plan ahead. That was obvious. Richard was the only stability I had ever had besides Mama Kate, Mama Gina, and Daddy Jim. I still got to visit them on weekends. I changed out of my bathing suit and put on some shorts, a shirt and tennis shoes. I was supposed to meet Stephanie at the fort. When I got there, she only had one cigarette, so we shared it. She said her mama was starting to miss the cigarettes so I told her I would grab a dollar out of Nancy Kate's purse, and we could walk to the store the next day and get cigarettes. The next day we met at the fort, and I showed her the dollar and a shoebox for our stash. Then we started to head to the store. She said, "I wish you hadn't got in a fight with the new boy. He's really cute and his mama won't let him near us now." I gave her a dirty look and her face turned red. Well now, she was starting to like these boys. How disgusting! I hated it when a boy and a girl liked each other because they got this really dumb look on their face, which Stephanie had right now. She looked like somebody hit her over the head with a hammer. What a traitor! I said, "Stephanie you're kicked out of the fort." She laughed and speaking of the devils, we passed the boys. They said, "what are y'all doing?" Stephanie said, "going to the store to buy cigarettes" and I elbowed her. They said, "you aren't old enough to buy cigarettes" and they just thought that was hilarious. We kept walking and I said, "just watch losers." When we got out of earshot, Stephanie said, "what are we gonna do?" I said, "when we walk in, I will ask you what kind of cigarettes your mama smokes and you just play along. You have to act casual." She said, "do you think it will work?" I said, "of course." As I pushed the door open, the bell rang and I called out to Stephanie, "Can we get gumballs too?" She said, "I don't know we have to get my mama's cigarettes and we may not have enough." I asked the lady behind the counter, "how much are cigarettes?" And she answered, "What kind?" I looked at Stephanie and she looked at the lady. She said, "they're called Eve, and they are in a green pack." The lady behind the counter said, "sixty-five cents and the gum balls are a penny each." She laid a dollar on the counter, and I said, "how many gum balls can we get?" She said twenty-five because of tax so I started counting out the gumballs and throwing them on the counter. There was a line behind us now. The lady gets the cigarettes and puts them in a bag with the gum balls and a pack of matches. Stephanie grabbed the bag, and we walked out clanging that bell again. I said, "Thank you Mam." Stephanie put a gum ball in her mouth and said, "I think we did mighty fine." I sarcastically said, "yeah we were brilliant, is that your damn mama pulling in?" We both took off running and ran all the way to the brick wall. We sat inside the bushes and caught our breath. I told Stephanie she had better go home, and I told her I would take the bag to the fort and put it in the shoebox. Just like a double knot spy, she said, "okay meet me at the clubhouse in the morning at 10 sharp" and then she took off. I got the bag and walked slowly towards the woods and there on the corner were the boys. I stopped, took the cellophane off the cigarettes, grabbed one, lit a match and inhaled. Then I continued to walk past the boys and towards the woods. They just stood there with their mouths open. When I got to the fort and climbed those crooked boards nailed into the tree, I sat the bag down and pulled myself in. It wasn't the fire tower, but it was better than nothing. I put everything in the shoebox except ten gum balls. I put them in my shorts pockets and started down the ladder. As I walked out of the woods, there were the boys. I said, "do yall want some gum balls?" and they said, "yes." I handed each of them a gum ball and walked towards home. They yelled, "what did you do with the cigarettes?" I yelled back, " I buried em just like I will bury all your sissy asses if you go looking for em."

When I walked into the condominium, Nancy Kate said I smelled like dirt and cigarettes. I told her Stephanie's mama smokes all the time and asked her if she wanted a gum ball. She stared at me and told me to go upstairs and take a shower. I told her I could go put my bathing suit on and go back to the pool. The pool would clean me right up. She started crying and mumbling about "all she wanted was a girl and she got four boys and me." She cried all the time. Mama Kate said she cried over spilled milk-literally. I said, "Alright stop you're howling I'm going." The week before school started, Mary Beth and Darlene came over. We had sleepovers every night but that would change to weekends when school started. We got to talking about their Catholic school and I asked them if they were from the North. Each of them had one parent from up North. So, I said, "what's it feel like to be half a Yankee?" They said they didn't like it because they didn't feel like they "belonged" to the North or the South. I said, "well it could be worse." And they asked me how. I said, "you could be a full-blown Yankee!" They both threw pillows at me, and I love a good pillow fight. It was on! Then I felt something strange. It felt like a liquid was coming out of me, but I wasn't peeing. I told them to hold up so I could go to the bathroom. When I went, I couldn't believe it. Blood was everywhere. I sat there and tried to figure out what was going on. I must be dying. Oh well! I stuffed toilet paper in there and pulled my shorts up. I ran out of the bathroom and told Mary Beth and Darlene I was bleeding to death. Instead of being worried, they were excited. They kept saying that I was the first one. Then they explained to me what a "period" was and said I had to call Nancy Kate and ask her to stop at the store and get something called "tampons." I called her and she said that "girls wear pads and ladies wear tampons." I said, "whatever." She wanted to talk about it, and I said "nope" and hung up. I told Mary Beth and Darlene to go home and find out everything they could from their parents about this situation and we would report to the clubhouse at noon tomorrow. I encouraged them to bring food and went to lay down. I didn't feel so good. This must be what your stomach feels like when you're having a baby. When Nancy Kate got home, you would have thought I was sure enough in the movie "Carrie." She starts talking about sex and how evil it is. Now what did that have to do with anything? I said, " how do you use this damn thing?" She told me and I took them and went into the bathroom. She was still running her mouth. I got straightened out and went to my room and closed the door. She was still talking so I turned the radio on loud. It was going to be a long night.

I met Mary Beth, and Darlene at the clubhouse, they had so much to tell me. When you get your period, if you have sex, you can have a baby now. Not a problem. I wasn't EVER having sex. The period would last for about seven days, it comes once a month and feels like someone is stabbing you in the stomach. They said to ask Nancy Kate for some aspirin for pain. So, they told me everything I needed to know and when Nancy Kate got home and tried to talk to me, I just said, "I need some aspirin for pain and some peace and quiet. I already know everything, and I don't want to hear another word about it." And that was that. On the bus ride to Lincoln Heights, there were mostly boys. Stephanie Smith was older, and she went to a different school also. One of the boys on the bus was David Hurt, Bill's grandson from nursery school. I think I bit him a few times. Now he had a crush on me. He would always tease me, and his face would turn red. And he would get that stupid look on his face and these googly eyes. Once we got to school, all the fifth graders had one teacher like Plaza Road. I cannot remember a thing about her. It was like an episode of Charlie Brown, she was up front saying, "whomp whomp whomp>whomp whomp whomp." We did schoolwork and during recess we played jacks, jumped rope, and played hopscotch. When we went outside there was a black girl that always wanted to fight with me, so we did every day. She just kept coming back for more like the energizer bunny. One day I tripped her, and she fell. I jumped on top of her and started punching her. All the kids stood in a circle and cheered us on. Then it got quiet, and I looked up. The teacher was standing there. She said, "Michelle Martin is going to the principal's office right now." So, I did but I took my time. It was my first time going to the principal's office and I wandered around and tried to get lost. No such luck, a lady found me and escorted me to the office. I sat outside and waited on a bench. Across from me were two twin black girls and one was beat up. I couldn't believe it. They had the same clothes on and looked exactly alike. They had been switching off on me. I wondered what it would be like to have a twin. I'm afraid I would be jealous of myself. The world couldn't take two of me. The principal opened the door. We all walked slowly in, and I didn't say a word. They both talked loud and fast, blaming everything on me of course. The principal looked at me and said, "and what do you have to say for yourself?" I said, "they fought me, and I fought back, so what's my punishment?" He said we would all get detention. I loved detention. I got to do all my homework and me and the twins got to be the best of friends. Their names were Monesha and

Tenesha. I called them Moe and T. They said they couldn't believe I was nice. Their mama told them white girls were stuck up and mean. I no longer got the free lunch ticket, so I gave them extra lunch money and they ate like they were starving. Their mama didn't care about them, and they didn't have a daddy. Their grandma had to take care of them and sometimes she didn't have enough money for food. Their mama didn't work, she did drugs and spent time with lots of men. Moe and T only had each other and now they had me. I listened to their stories and brought them things from home they needed. When detention was over, I missed them and tried to see them but my days at school were changing. The teacher told me I would be moved to a special class for "gifted" students because when I finished my work, I disrupted the entire class, and she couldn't have that. The new class had only a few nerds in it, and they were all boys. We had bright colored puzzles to put together and we made up our own learning schedule. We read, did classroom work, there was no homework and if we finished early, there were more puzzles, games, and activities. It was fun. Before I knew it the school year was over, and it was time to leave Candlewood. I never wanted to leave. I wanted to stay there forever, but it was time to start all over again

CHAPTER 5 THE NEW GIRL

The new house we moved into was built just for us and it was in a good neighborhood called "Birnam Woods." Each street name had an association with Shakespeare. The name of our street was "Portia Place." The house was an "A" framed ranch house, and my bedroom and Michael's bedroom were on one side of the house and Richard and Nancy Kate's bedroom was on the other side. Outside was a sunroom and spacious backyard leading to a wooded area with trails. The next-door neighbor had a fenced in backyard with a giant shaggy dog. We got a dog too and his name was Charlie. He was a black cockapoo. Nancy Kate let me get him because she thought it was "trendy." Charlie had seizures but by this time, working with animals was second nature so I gave him his medicine and tried to stay calm when he had seizures which, thankfully, weren't that often. The seizure medicine helped a great deal, and I had Richard to thank for that. I knew I had to be careful with animals around Nancy Kate, she could be cruel to them. I should have realized then, when she wasn't being cruel, it was an act. Charlie and I explored the neighborhood and found a creek behind the house. It would turn into a beautiful ice pond in the dead of winter. The trails led to Waverly Swim Club which we ended up joining later that year.

My first day of school was unlike any other in my life. This school was near the house and the name of it was "Hickory Grove Elementary School." The teacher was a young black woman, and all the kids were white. I thought we were supposed to be bused around Charlotte. They forgot this school. I learned later that most of the kids lived in the "Grove Park" community aka "The Grove." The boys in "The Grove" were considered very cool and were called "The Grove Boys." The teacher called me in front of the class and introduced me. That was genuinely nice of her. I was glad she didn't ask me to speak. Everyone in the class stared at me and I felt like a movie star. I went to my desk and observed people throughout the day. They kept glancing at me. I immediately noticed that these kids were different. I wouldn't say they were "goody two shoes" but they had led a very sheltered life. They all had nice, normal families with a mother and a father, and this is the only school they had ever been to, except for "Timmy Detter." Timmy Deter went to Plaza Road Elementary with me so at least I knew one kid. All eyes followed me around throughout the day and they all whispered to each other. They were very polite to me, which I got a huge kick out of. This school was going to be "a piece of cake."

When I got home, I went through Nancy Kate's makeup. If everyone was going to give me this much attention, I would have to look my best. I took foundation and face powder which makes your face look flawless. Later I added blush and mascara. Then I eventually graduated to heavy eyeliner and lip gloss. After that, I was the "shizit." My hair was long and straight so all I had to do was brush it. I didn't like curly hair on me, but it looked good on some people. As I got to know the kids at school, I realized that most of them were very smart. I was more than a little shocked and became competitive in my schoolwork. I hung around with the smart girls which were-Carolina Martin, Teresa Farmer, and Charlotte Almond. Caroline lived in Birnam Woods, and I would visit her house so we could study together. Caroline had the perfect life. She had a big white house with a pool and both of her parents loved each other. Down the street from Caroline was Tammy Hammer's house. Tammy was tougher than the other kids and we became the best of friends. She had a trampoline and we bounced on it every day and talked about school. Tammy told me about a boy in school that she liked, and his name was Mark Brown. She said all the girls liked him and he had always been the most popular and best-looking boy in school. She told me where he sat so I promised her I would check him out the next day. So, as promised, the following day, when I got to school and sat in my seat I turned to my left and counted two seats. There sat the most beautiful boy I had ever seen. He had dark hair, an olive complexion and a smile that lit up the room. I know because he turned around and smiled at me. I had never liked a boy before, and I couldn't stop looking at him. Now making fun of Stephanie Smith didn't seem so funny. My face and neck were flushed red, and my stomach tingled. No wonder everyone made such a big deal about this. The entire day I felt vulnerable. He kept turning around and smiling at me and I kept turning red. This was horrible. I decided not to tell Tammy. She saw him first. After school she asked me about him and I said, "oh yeah he's kind of cute. Does he like you?" She said she didn't know, and I felt a stab of relief. I had to remember that Tammy was my best friend and I had to be loyal to her. But if for some reason they didn't work out, I would be there to console him. I mean her.

After that I got distracted anyway by the classroom bully. His name was "Floyd Tipton", and he was constantly picking on me. I was trying to get a fresh start and fit in, but Tammy Hammer advised me to punch him in the face. Day after day, when we went outside for recess he would throw dodge balls at my head, spit on me and try to trip me. One day he walked up and smacked me right in the head and I looked over at the teacher. I did not want to go to the principal's office, so I went and sat in my seat. I was so mad that I was close to crying. Then the teacher said that she wanted to talk to me and pointed to the door. I followed her to a conference room and by then, tears were running down my face. She went and got some Kleenex, but I really needed a towel. She told me that she had been watching Floyd torture me every day and she wanted to talk to me about it. "Do you know why Floyd treats you this way?" I said, "because he hates my guts." And she said, "No, the opposite." She explained to me that boys mature slower than girls and when they want attention, sometimes they act in a bad way. The reason he was doing all these things was to get my attention because he had a crush on me. My mouth dropped open and I took a big gulp of air in. Could this be true? The teacher knew everything, so it had to be. I asked her what I should do. She said, "think of it as a superpower that you have over boys and use it to your advantage." When I asked her how, she told me that no matter what Floyd did to me, to just smile at him and talk sweetly to him and see what happens. When I walked back to my seat, I felt like a new person. This information was life changing. The next time Floyd Tipton hit me, I looked him right in the eyes and blinked and smiled. He almost fell over. From that day forward, the tables were turned. I was extra sweet to him and tried to give him attention and he became terrified of me. I could look at him and smile and it was like someone slapping him across the face. He was totally under my spell and the teacher must have noticed because one day, she winked at me. I didn't know how to wink back yet so I just smiled big as if to say, "thank you." Between looking at Mark and Floyd all day, it was hard to get any work done.

Then everyone started talking about the annual Spelling Bee. I didn't know what that was, but Caroline told me about it. It was important. How do you study for a spelling bee, read the dictionary? No matter how hard I tried I couldn't be bothered with it, until that day came. One at a time people were called in front of the class to spell words. When I got up there, I just spelled the word and waited for the time when I would get it wrong, but I never did. The next thing I knew there were two of us left, me and Jeff Borders-the smartest boy in the class. I really wished I had read that dictionary. If I didn't win, everyone would make a big deal of it, so I tried hard. I sounded out each word and we kept going back and forth until he spelled a word wrong. I just looked around like, what next? Apparently if I spelled the next word right, I was the winner. And I did. The classroom went crazy. I was excited. When I told Nancy Kate, she just gave me a blank stare and rolled her eyes. I guess they didn't have Spelling Bees in Anson County. Towards the end of the school year, we had to take a test.

This test was to see how smart you were compared to other kids in your grade. I loved to take tests but not this one. They were using it to "label" us and I didn't like it, until the results came back. In every category I was on the twelfth-grade level so I wondered if I could quit school now. Again, I went home and showed Nancy Kate the results. First of all, she was not smart enough to comprehend the results and I had to explain them to her. Secondly, she could have cared less. I always got straight A's and she never acknowledged that in any way. It was around this time that I started to resent Nancy Kate. Michael was starting to get curious about why I would visit Mama Gina and Daddy Jim and he didn't. It wasn't my place to tell him the truth and I wanted to kick her, not because of what she did but because she never told Michael the truth. He deserved to know the truth and maybe even meet his dad. I cried when I thought about it. To me my brothers were Michael, Kerry, and Robin. Kevin was just a smaller version of Nancy Kate. Me and Kerry called him "Little Nancy."

Then Nancy Kate had a brilliant idea. She decided to send me to Troy Anne Ross Institute of Modeling. It would be on the weekend so I wouldn't miss school. She said that I was going to "learn how to be a lady." I had to dress up and go to South Charlotte every weekend and I felt like "Ellie Mae Clampett." I learned to stand, talk, walk, sit, and act. I hated going but I did love the part about "how to apply makeup." There was more to it than I thought. You have to "prime" your face like painting a wall. There were ways to "shadow" your flaws and "highlight" your assets. The main reason I hated going is because all the girls there were the prettiest, richest, and most stuck-up girls in Charlotte. And that's no joke. They were straight up snobs. I couldn't even talk to them because I had nothing in common with them. I just learned each lesson and ignored them. Some of these girls needed a "bitch slap" but ignoring them was worse in their minds. I didn't realize it then but the lessons I learned in modeling school were invaluable in many ways. I didn't just learn how to be a lady, but I learned to NEVER look down on other people. I was glad when I graduated with a photo shoot and modeling show but only because I knew it was over.

Mama Kate was not doing well, and Nancy Kate sent her to a nursing home. Mama Kate should have come to stay with us. There was no reason she should have to go to a nursing home. She hated it there and always looked sad now. Her long hair was cut short, and her eyes were filled with sadness. She had told me she was afraid of dying and so was I. I wanted to be with her and help her get better, so I started writing her long letters to cheer her up. The last one I wrote came back to me in the mail- "deceased." I called Nancy Kate and she said she was going to tell me that Mama Kate died. I hung up and screamed as loud as I could. I cried like a baby and poor Michael didn't know what to do. I was heartbroken. I opened the letter and read it, realizing that Mama Kate had never gotten the chance to. **TURN THE PAGE**

CHAPTER 6 KEEPER OF THE NISHIKIGOI

I'm not sure how I became "The Koi Fish Keeper." It all started with a sad, slow turn of events in the dreaded year of 2020. I loved living on the plantation, but I knew I was there for a reason, especially when the pandemic hit. When I pulled into the gate, I was protected in seclusion, but I could still see on the news that there was death and destruction taking place all over the world. Some people wanted to start a race war but there was no time for that. People were struggling to survive. At this point, it was the world against the virus, and it did not discriminate. The description of COVID-19 reminds me of Eosinophilic Asthma. I remember once thinking in anger that I wished everyone could empathize and feel what it was like to suffer from asthma. I wished everyone could feel what it was like to fight for each breath. Now it was coming true, and I wanted to take it all back. I didn't want other people to suffer just because I was. I had to get a monthly shot and when the pandemic hit, the mail stopped coming. I didn't get my shot for two months, so I had to call the ambulance twice and use both of my epi-pens. I called and raised CANE to get my shots back started and it must have worked because I got extra. These shots were $15,000 a piece but a pharmaceutical assistance program paid for them. I always immediately refrigerated the shots and saved them because they were my lifeline, and I knew it. I isolated myself as much as possible. As I looked out the window of the cottage, there was a storm brewing. I watched the trees as they bent sideways. I was in awe of the force of nature. The trees were resilient, but the wind was powerful. I felt a sense of dread. Without the wind, trees wouldn't shed their dead branches. Without the wind, the tree's roots wouldn't build up enough strength to hold up the tree. I closed the blinds and braced for the storm. It was time to build up my roots.

There were rumors in town that my dad was sick with liver disease. My brother Kevin was the only one in the family still talking to him. I didn't realize at the time, but that was how he planned it. I called Kevin and asked him if dad was sick and he reassured me that he was fine, repeatedly. One day me and Kerry were driving down Highway 52 and I said, "let's stop and see dad." He reluctantly agreed. When we went in, my dad was alone in his recliner gasping for his breath. I wanted to call an ambulance, but he refused. It was obvious that he was dying. Kerry and I got to talk to him, and we both knew it would be the last time. He wouldn't let us help him and called Kevin. When Kevin got there, we told my dad goodbye and walked to the kitchen. Tears were streaming down my face and Kevin walked in-grinning from ear to ear. This is the day he had waited for all his life. He had been a slave to my dad. He had given up his hopes and dreams to satisfy my dad. To me, success was making a difference in the world and earning your own money. To him, success was waiting on someone to die and give you money. I was disgusted. When Kerry and I got in the car, he said, "stop crying!" Then we talked about how bad dad was and we felt helpless. He was brainwashed and we didn't know it at the time but he had dementia. There wasn't anything we could do. I called Robin to tell him, and he sent his son, Derek, to say his goodbyes. Derek asked my dad if he wanted to see Robin and he said he didn't. A few days later, Kerry got a call from 1-800. 1-800's real name is Franklin Gibson. When we were teenagers-me, 800 and Kevin went to a club in Rockingham. Whenever 800 saw a girl he liked, he would say, "just call 1-800 Franklin Gibson. Franklin Gibson at your service." From then on, we just called him 1-800. If 800 had not called that day, me and Kerry would never know what happened on Tuesday, March 17th, 2020. My dad went to meet Saint Patrick himself. I'm sure right before he died, he realized the truth. As he lay in bed upstairs calling out in pain, one of Kevin's flunkies sat downstairs and turned the TV up. Two days later, it got quiet, and a call was made to Kevin to tell him the good news. That's why I cried, but not in front of Kerry. I kept picturing this in my head. I rode over to dad's house to confront Kevin, and Kerry pulled up. I walked over to Kerry, and he said, "what are you doing here?" I said, "what are you doing here?" He said, "same thing you are, come on." We both walked over to Kevin and started questioning him. Then Kerry looked at me and said, "do you have your damn pajamas on?" I looked at him and said, "are you just now noticing?" He rolled his eyes and we both started in on Kevin again. Kevin calmed us down and told us about the viewing and the funeral. He said dad did not suffer. Kerry and I both left wondering how Kevin could do this.

Kerry must have called Kevin every hour on the hour. Kevin called me for the first time in my life to tell me to "stop telling Kerry to call me!" I didn't know what he was talking about, I was busy making my own plans for Kevin. He had waited for this funeral all his life and I was about to make it special. With COVID, funerals were supposed to be only for family. The only person I invited to the viewing was Kevin's ex-wife Janet. My dad looked good in his expensive casket. His cowboy hat was laying on top.

At one time, my dad and I were close. I tried to remember that time. For fifteen years, every Sunday after dinner (that's lunch for city folks, last meal is supper) we would go horseback riding and "get up cows." I would ride Buster and he would ride Champ. When Champ got older, he switched to Rowdy Monkey. Sometimes Brandi would ride, and she was exceptionally good. She had riding lessons and took to horses as she did all animals. Sandra Wellman and I were still friends after all these years and she would ride. The first time my dad met Sandra he put her on Champ to "show the city girl how it was done" but Sandra was originally from Texas and she rode like a champ. He was impressed and after that, he loved having her with us. I lived with my dad for years when he was married to his third wife, Faye. When my dad got sick, Kevin started to isolate him from the rest of the family.

When I got to the funeral, Robin was standing away from the gravesite next to a tree. Me, Robin, and Kerry should have been in the front row at the gravesite where chairs were lined up under the tent. Instead, there sat a row of ugly ass women. I walked up in front of them and shouted, "all you whores need to sit in the back." The expression on their faces and Kevin's face was priceless. One looked scared. One appeared to faint. I think Kerry was giggling. Others tried to talk to me, and I continued, "whores to the back, all whores to the back." My nephew and his wife came and grabbed me by the arm and pulled me away. I walked up to Robin, and we were both crying. Then I walked back to my car and left. I stopped at my dad's to get one of his hats as a keepsake. For the first time ever in my life, the doors were locked. Kevin had people sitting outside in cars "guarding the house." Kevin's daughter Charity pulled up and I hugged her. Her dad had not bothered to call her. Kerry called her. I told her what just happened, and she said she wasn't going then.

A few days later, I got my second call from Kevin. He was angry and asked me why I did that. I asked him why he cared and said he must be a whore too. He was angrier. He told me and Kerry that we were to meet him at dad's house Saturday at noon for the reading of the will. I knew then that me and Kerry were not in the will, but I wanted a copy of it. When I got there on Saturday, the entire Anson County Sheriff's department was there. Hmmm. Nana was right. Kevin feared me and Kerry. I got out and Kevin said I couldn't come into the house because I might have COVID. I told him to hand me a copy of the will. He said no. Kerry was late and he made me wait on him. I waited in the car. A sheriff's deputy walked up, and I rolled the electric window down. He said, "Kevin says you have COVID." I said, "No. Tell Kevin," I said- he looks like his mama." He grinned and said, "sorry about this, it happens more than you know." I nodded and Kerry pulled up. I got out and once again asked Kevin to hand me a copy of the will. He said that it would be read to me. Flunkie number two started to read the will and I realized Kevin didn't know how to read. He handed me a copy. I glanced down and saw that Kerry, Robin and I were cut out of the will, and I turned around to leave. Kevin said, "No, no you have to hear it." I kept going. He called my name and said, "Come here and sit down. I've got something to say." as he pointed to the brick wall. I walked over and sat on the brick wall next to Kerry looking up at him and giving him my full attention. The officers were lined up against the wall watching this like a bad reality show. Kevin put his hands in the air and said, "All this is mine and you are never welcome here again." Me and Kerry looked at each other and laughed. I knew exactly what Kerry was thinking. I was thinking of something else. I was thinking Don had all that money and talent and was as humble as he could be. This fool has a pig farm and some land and thinks he is a Rockefeller. I went home and put the will on the refrigerator with a magnet. Kerry was right behind me, mad as a hornet. I said, "Kerry, you cannot kill him because you would go back to prison." He hesitated and said that he was going to make copies and put them on all the telephone poles in Anson County. As he walked out, I said, "don't forget the post office." I picked up the will and read it again, " to my daughter Michelle and my two sons Kerry and Robin, I leave nothing." This made it so much easier to grieve.

But I didn't have much time for grief before the next epic event. Brandi was already having a relapse, so I was very anxious, but her dad was taking care of her, thank goodness. He was trying to get her into an excellent rehab facility in California called "Hope by the Sea." I decided to forget about everything and go to Sandra Wellman's birthday party. A friendship that lasted fifty years was worth celebrating. Kerry called and said to stop by his house which was near Sandra's. He wouldn't tell me why. When I stopped by and saw him, I knew it was bad, but I did not have a clue how bad. Unfortunately for both of us, Kerry and I were like twins. We were so attached, if one of us were sick, the other would get sick. Sometimes I would try to create distance between us so that we would not develop an unhealthy dependence on each other. I knew Kerry wasn't doing well but I was trying to survive myself. Robin moved on and took it all in stride.

Kerry was just skin and bones. He was shaking and said he had something to tell me. He told me not to be alarmed but the police were coming to pick him up any minute and he needed me to "tie up some loose ends." I looked over at his pit bull tied to a tree and knew that he would be the first thing I took care of. I had already been coming over to feed, water and check on him. I followed him into the house, and he raced around grapping papers and prescription bottles and handing them to me. He handed me the keys to his truck, car, and motorcycle. When I asked him why he started to talk in circles, it didn't make any sense. I looked at the bottle and it said "oxycontin." I said, "are you hooked on these?" He said, " yes I've been hooked on them for years." I took everything and told him I would be back the next day. I went to Sandra's party and had a wonderful time. Sometimes when terrible things happen, I just block them out and keep going. It caught up with me the next morning. I called Robin and Nana and told them I was coming over to talk to them in person because I couldn't talk about the situation on the phone. (Kerry said the phones were tapped) Now most people wouldn't believe him but at one time, he did have his phones tapped and he went to prison. He flew to Brazil to live for a few years to fight extradition. A brilliant attorney told him he should do that. Anywho, I went to Robin's and told him what Kerry said and asked him if he could find a loving home for the dog. He said he would. Then I went to Nana's and told her what was going on. She screamed, cried, and called Michael. I took her with me but that was a mistake. While Robin found a home for the dog and transported him, I took Kerry to the hospital. This is where it gets complicated.

I was already dealing with other issues. Years ago, Kerry and I both experienced severe back pain at the exact same time. Mine was sciatic nerve pain and his was on the upper right side of his back near his spine. I eventually had emergency back surgery for a ruptured disc. Afterwards, for the second time in my life, I developed Post Traumatic Stress Disorder. It was harder to recover from the surgery mentally than it was physically. I kept having flash backs of the pain. The lights were too bright. The sounds were too loud, and I would suffer from phantom pains. I could feel the arterial disc in my back, and I thought it was making me sick. PTSD is no joke.

While I was having my surgery, Kerry's doctor got him hooked on pain medicine. There is a huge opiate crisis in North Carolina and there are no resources to help people. When they took his blood at the hospital, the nurse said he had enough oxycontin in his system to tranquilize a horse.

Nana was in the car because "she didn't want anyone to steal her car" and "she didn't want to be around sick people." She also had dementia but we didn't know it at the time. They gave him something for his symptoms and released him. Robin and I tried to get him into rehab but there was always an excuse not to take him. He had a criminal record. There was a waiting list. One even said, "you have to get him off the pills before we can take him." Wait, what? Isn't that the purpose of rehab?

Michael, Robin, and I were also trying to take care of Nana, but no one could stand to be around her. She just had her third seizure in a year and this time she hit a tree and totaled her car. She wasn't supposed to drive but she did anyway. Not only was she putting her life in danger but others as well. A narcissist only thinks of themselves, and her mental problems were getting much worse. She could not keep up with her lies. We were trying to get the medical Power of Attorney over her so we could talk to the doctor and find out what was wrong. She would never tell the truth and we didn't know what was wrong with her. We didn't have a clue what medicines she was taking or not taking. She kept telling us she didn't have a seizure disorder, her jaw was "out of whack." There were many things "out of whack" with her, not just her jaw.

In the middle of the next night, Kerry called me at 3 a.m. and said he was lying on the side of the road in Monroe on Highway 74. He had called an ambulance, and the Emergency Room kicked him out after they found out he didn't have insurance. This was unbelievable. I told him I would be right there. I picked him up and the nighttime quickly turned into daytime. I took him to different rehabs and none of them would take him. I finally dropped him off at this house and told him to try and get some sleep. The next morning, I would have to take Nana to her doctor's appointment.

I picked her up at the Senior Living Apartments and we took her car. She wasn't allowed to drive but got a new car on the internet. I'm not sure what meds she took but she was crying and cursing about Kerry. I was tired, hungry and on autopilot. I went through the drive-through and asked her if she wanted anything and she said that she didn't. As soon as I pulled off and tried to take a bite of my chicken biscuit, she yanked the steering wheel and started screaming, " you can't eat in my new car. This is my car. This is my car." I pulled over and put the car in the park, wrapped the biscuit up and told her not to say another word. She knew she had gone too far. My temper even scares me. Whenever she tried to talk, I would shout, "not a word!" We drove in silence. I had reached my breaking point, and PTSD was kicking in. I saw flashes of light and memories of asthma attacks and back pain came flooding back.

When I pulled up to her doctor's office, I put on a mask, and we walked in. I wanted to tell the receptionist immediately what I was there for because I did not want to waste any time. As I started to talk to her, she ignored me and began to ask COVID questions. Then Nana interrupted and said, "I've changed my mind. I am not signing any papers for you today." She was not giving me medical Power of Attorney. The nurse snapped, "I have to have these questions answered now." I pulled off my mask, threw it on the floor and told them both to "have a nice day." Then I turned, walked out, got in the car, grabbed my chicken biscuit and coke. I shoved that chicken biscuit in my mouth and chugged that coke as I drove away. Then I threw the trash in the back seat. When I got to her apartment, I parked, threw the keys in the front seat, and went to my car. I went home, turned my phone off and slept for the next 24 hours. When I woke up, I called Robin and told him it was his turn. I was done. He said he understood and would take over. After that I tried to concentrate on healing myself. Then a few days later, Don died. I was heartbroken. I had just talked to him. He was the most stable person in my life and now he was gone. I grabbed a bottle of wine, a glass, put the music on my phone and walked down to the dock off the pond. I sat there and drank. And I cried.

After a few weeks, everything on the plantation started to die. The green and blue lights all over the property stopped coming on at night. Helena, Mario, and Marcio were gone. The fruit and flowers in the garden were dead. The grass needed cutting and when I walked by the Koi Pond, there were three dead fish floating on top of the water. There were fifty fish in this pond, and I was not going to let them all die. I went to the storage building to see if there was anything in there for them and I found their food. I took the dead fish out with a net and fed the remaining fish. The next day, there were two more dead fish floating on top of the water. They were all at the surface and seemed to be gasping for air. I called Nana and asked her what to do. She said, "just let those damn fish die." Then I remembered why I wasn't talking to her. I talked to other people, did my research, and went to Lowe's and PetSmart. I bought pumps, filters, food, watercolor, algae killer, and barley. One day Mario came by, and he helped me set up the pumps and filter. Koi fish need oxygen and bubbles, so I had three pumps in case pumps one and two stopped working. The electricity didn't work, and Mario helped me find a plug. They can't have regular water because of the chlorine. Don had two barrels of rainwater and I added rainwater to the pond to get their water cleaned out. By the time I finished, it was even more beautiful than before and the koi fish started to thrive. Koi is a homophone for another word that means " love" and the koi fish are a universal symbol of peace. They are a bright, vivid, ornamental fish that represent success, ambition, perseverance, and advancement in life. All these characteristics reminded me of Don. Their modest behavior and elegant movement put my mind at peace. They were "swimming jewels."

I glanced around the rest of the plantation. The colorful chickens were gone. Mario had taken them away. Don's dog "Oscar" went to a new home. Statues were covered by leaves. The pool cover was filled with water. And the Oak trees were shedding their dead branches. But there in the middle of it all, was the peaceful beauty of the koi pond. And that's how I became "The Koi Fish Keeper," or "Keeper of the Nishikigoi." TURN THE PAGE

If you are the desert, I'll be the sea

If you're ever hungry, hunger for me

Whatever you ask for, that's what I'll be

So, when you remember the ones who have lied,

who said that they cared but then laughed as you cried,

Beautiful Darling, don't think of me, cause all I ever wanted

I will be your Father Figure;

I will be the one who loves you until the end of time

George Michael

CHAPTER 7 FORTUNATE ONE

Dun do Dun do Dun do Dun do.

(sound of choppers)

Some folks are born made to wave the flag

They are red, white, and blue

And when the band plays "Hail to the Chief"

They point the cannon at you, Lord

It Ain't Me, It Ain't Me

I ain't no senator's son, son

It Ain't Me, It Ain't Me

I ain't no fortunate one

Some folks are born silver spoon in hand

Lord, don't they help themselves, yeah

But when the taxman comes to the door

House lookin like a rummage sale

It Ain't Me, It Ain't Me, I ain't no senator's son, son

It Ain't Me, It Ain't Me, I ain't no fortunate one

Creedance Clearwater Revival

Over time I started seeing my father more. Mama Gina would take me to the "sale barn" or "cattle auction barn" where he worked. She helped in the office sometimes and I would go help the boys' run cows into pens. I watched my dad with what looked like hedge clippers, or bolt cutters and he used them to cut the teeth out of Boars. Blood would squirt everywhere, and they would squeal. It was dusty, smelly, and hot. I liked to run the cows but every once and awhile, there would be a bull that did not move. The first time this happened, I went forward, and he didn't budge. He just stared me down. Well, I took another step and so did he, then I made a run for it as he charged me. I went up the wooden fence and over, just as his horns started stabbing the fence. The boys were laughing until my dad walked up and told them to "get that bull up now!" I stood aside and watched and did not dare crack a smile. My dad seemed to get used to me. I couldn't tell how he felt really. He rarely showed emotion, like a "Clint Eastwood character." There is one thing that could not be denied. He was tough. He had broken bones and had bruises all over on a regular basis. After a while, we all did. The physical scars were never as bad as the mental ones though.

Mama Gina took me to watch him play baseball. I'm not even sure if he knew I was there. I watched him hit home run after home run and wondered if there was anything he couldn't do. Later I would learn to help on the ranch. We would put a bull in the shoot, he would slam the metal bar down over his neck, I would jump on the bull backwards, grab his tail as hard as I could and pull back. Then he would walk to the back with a razor blade and castrate the bull. Nothing phased him. Even when we "pulled" calves, if they didn't make it, he was only disappointed because of the money that would be lost.

When Mama Gina was growing up in Ansonville, her father, "Bop" owned the General Store in town and was rich. He got rich from bartering, selling goods and renting out his properties. Whenever people owed money on their taxes and couldn't pay them, he would go to the courthouse, pay the taxes, and take their land, farm, and house. Then he would charge people rent to live in what used to be their home. Mama said Bop loved me. There was a picture of me sitting on his lap and he had a big smile on his face. I was looking up at him.

When Mama Gina married Daddy Jim, he was a bootlegger. He ran moonshine back and forth across the state line during The Prohibition. As slow as he drove, that was hard to believe. Rumor has it, Daddy Jim wasn't always the Big Teddy Bear he was to me. I guess that's why my dad was so tough, but the bottom line is: my dad swindled the rest of the family out of their share of the money, and he ended up with everything. He was greedy. If you needed to borrow a dime, he wouldn't lend it to you. That applied to his kids as well. When me and my brothers worked cattle all day long, our payment was food on the table and a roof over our head for that night. That was the deal, and we knew it. Kerry and Robin would come to Charlotte to visit mom. Kerry finally told Michael the truth. We all knew that all we had was each other, except for Kevin. Kevin was only out for himself.

For where your treasure is,

there will be your heart also

Matthews: 6:21

After Mama Kate died, school was out for the summer. Tammy Hammer and I started going to Waverly Swim Club every day. Michael and his friends went too. I was getting the best tan I ever had. There were so many kids there to play with and no lifeguards. The best swimmers were Bob Morgan and Kit Young. They were on the swim team. I guess I had a little crush on them. This was when I started sleepwalking. I went to sleep thinking about laying out by the pool with my dark tan as Bob Morgan swam by me. When I woke up, I was standing outside in my pajamas on the front lawn. I went to the front door, and it was locked so I rang the doorbell. The porch light came on and Mama said, "what are you doing outside?" I looked down at my bare feet and said, "I don't know." She talked about tying me to my bed and I really hoped she was kidding. The next day, my perfect summer ended. All of us kids were trying to "rock the pool." One by one, as fast as we could climb the high dive board, run to the end, and jump off and run back to the ladder. The pool would start rocking like the sea in an angry storm. We had the pool rocking great and as I reached the top of the ladder; I slipped backwards and fell onto the cement below. You could hear a loud "crack" and then everything turned dark. When I opened my eyes, I couldn't move, and people were standing around me. Tammy Hammer's dad said, "call an ambulance!" He put some type of blanket or jacket on me. I kept hearing his voice go in and out as he told me to stay awake. I don't remember the ambulance ride but when I woke up in the hospital, I was embarrassed to be in my bathing suit. The doctor was calm and said, "wow, what a great tan!" Then he asked me to move parts of my body one at a time. When it came to my left arm, I couldn't move it. As I wondered if he was getting ready to lecture me about "the dangers of the sun," he said he was ordering an x-ray of my left side. He thought my left arm might be broken. It ended up being my shoulder. I still had to wear a cast, but I was just thrilled because I got to pick the color. I picked bright pink. The cast was to weigh my shoulder down so it would "set" right. I had to sleep in a chair at night which meant I didn't sleep. I was starting to have trouble sleeping at night anyway. I still went to Waverly every day. I took a big, black marker and had everyone sign my cast. By the time I got it off, it was time to go back to school and Tammy Hammer was moving away. Everything was changing. We would all be bused to a different school called J.T. Williams. It was in the ghetto and there were rumors about riots and racial tension. I wasn't sure how my newest classmates were going to survive Junior High School, but they surprised me. They were tougher than I thought. Caroline and I rode Bus #37, and The Grove Boys rode bus #57. We would stand at the bus stop in the dark each morning- freezing- and then ride an hour to get to school. There was a boy named Charlie Brown on our bus and he was rowdy. Charlie, Jeff Borders, and Scott Pace would run around, fight, yell, and spit on cars. By the time we got to school, I felt like it should be the end of the day. If you looked out the window, things looked just like they did when I went to Lincoln Heights.

Even though the news said how hard it was for black and white people to get along, we didn't seem to notice. We all just accepted each other and didn't think much of it. This seemed to be a "grown up thing." We each had our own lockers and went the same routes to classes each day. The routine became familiar and after school all of us girls would go to softball practice and/or games. We played for Hickory Grove Presbyterian Church. There was a group of us who all hung out together from school plus Tina Johnston, she went to a private school that year. Tina and I became good friends, and I would walk to her house and then we would walk the rest of the way to the softball field. If there was a game, we would take a bus to the game. Instead of the "Bad News Bears" we were the "Badass Bears." Everyone on the team was good. I usually played second base or short stop along with Tina and Susan Hinson. Our coaches were Bobby and Kevin. They were young, handsome and didn't have a clue what they were getting themselves into. We were always fighting, whether it was each other or the other team.

There were a few things about this school year that I will never forget. My English teacher wore lots of makeup that seemed to drip down her face. She was unlike anyone I had ever met before and treated me like an adult. Once we were talking about a book and the subject of religion and the bible came up. She nonchalantly said that she didn't believe in the bible. She said it was just a myth, like the myths in Greek mythology. I was dumbfounded. At first, I felt sorry for her, but then I wondered if she might be right. She said, "read the whole bible Michelle, it is full of contradictions." So, I began to read the bible, a few chapters a day every day until I had read it cover to cover. Honestly, it didn't always make sense to me, and doubts crept into my mind.

My science teacher was Mr. Chandler and he had jars of dead things in formaldehyde all over his room, including a fetus. Being in his classroom was creepy to me and I was disgusted when he told us we would be dissecting frogs. I thought about Mama Gina's "hoppy toads", and she would not be pleased. I was on the school paper and our Journalism teacher was by far the oddest of them all. He looked like Ichabod Crane from "the Headless Horseman." He was skinny with a large pointy nose and dark hair. He stuttered and walked around constantly talking while waving his arms around in a dramatic fashion. I was fascinated by his flamboyant speeches.

No one was allowed in the halls without a hall pass and the rules were strict there. It was like we were in a prison on lock down. (I saw that on tv) There was a covered metal bridge that crossed over the highway, and we were not allowed to go near it. So of course, that is what I couldn't wait to do. I wanted to skip class and cross the bridge to see what was on the other side. No one wanted to do it with me so, one day I did it by myself. After the bell rang, everyone started towards their classes, and I walked like I was going to class. When the walkways and halls were empty, I ran to the bridge and made it inside. When I looked back, no one came after me. When I looked down, I could see cars racing by. It seemed like it took forever to cross the metal and cement bridge. I thought it was like a book I read called, "The Lion, The Witch and the Wardrobe." by C.S. Lewis. The other side had a parallel universe. The experience itself reminded me of being in the fire tower across from Mama Gina's house, because of the way the wind rattled the steel and made a loud noise. When I got to the other side, I peeked out, hoping to find some snow and a talking lion, but instead there were rows of little white houses with dirt for yards instead of grass. It looked like a poor, abandoned village. I started to walk down the street and a black man came out of a house and stood there staring at me, just like that bull. I stopped and stared back at him. Thoughts raced through my mind. I remembered that bull charging me, and I knew I was about to get into trouble. So, I turned, but instead of running, I skipped back to the bridge like I was playing a game. I turned back and he was still staring at me. I waved and ran back across the bridge. That must have taken longer than I thought because when I went to hang out in the bathroom, not long after that, the next bell rang. I went to class and now I knew why they called it "skipping class." It never worried me to "miss" class because I could go one day and keep up. Another time, when I skipped school, I decided to go to the store. I walked past the buses and down the road to the store. When I went inside there was a black woman behind the counter, and she was arguing with another black woman. They ignored me and I looked around. There was a jar of pig's feet, some eggs in pink juice and frog's legs. It reminded me of science class, and I felt like I was going to throw up. I went back outside and went back to school. I had satisfied my curiosity. No more skipping school at J.T. Williams.

The last thing I remember about that year is, I had a friend in English class named Frank. When we had "teacher's workday" he was going on a train to visit some relatives. He was excited about it. I remembered riding on a train to Spartanburg S.C. for a field trip one time, but this was a train where you spent the night. I was impressed. But when we came back to school, Frank never returned. His train had derailed, and a refrigerator fell on him. He was the only person on the train that died. I couldn't believe it. When the English teacher told us, she looked sad like she would cry. I wondered what she thought happened to people after they died, so at recess I asked her. She said, "there is no life after death. You just turn to dust. Frank is gone forever." Her words echoed in my mind throughout the day. If she was right, Mama Kate was gone forever too. **TURN THE PAGE**

CHAPTER 8 QUE SERA SERA

I remember watching every Doris Day movie I could find on TV. My favorites were the ones with Rock Hudson. What on-screen chemistry they had, or so I thought. My romantic fantasy of a perfect love was shattered when I read her autobiography. Her personal life was plagued with personal tragedy and was not at all like the carefree girl next door she played in her movies. Her relationship with Rock Hudson was not at all romantic, but it was a great friendship. She had been through failed marriages, personal struggles and her second husband- Martin Melcher, squandered her fortune. There were certain things we had in common. For instance, she was a true animal lover and rescued many animals through her foundation. After her career, she devoted her life to saving animals and the tranquility of nature.

I considered my second year of Junior High School, my "Doris Day" year. It all started with my French class. I wanted to take French because I was intrigued by the French version of The Beatle's song, "Michelle" which I was named after.

Michelle, ma belle

C'est toujours ainsi que je t'apelle

Michelle, ma belle

Sont des mots qui vont tres bien ensemble

Tres bien ensemble

Je t'aime Je t'aime Je t'aime

C'est tout ce que je sais jusqua l'instant reve

Ou ton coeur dans ces trois mots de'couvrira mon amour

Michelle, ma belle

Sont des mot qui vont tres bien ensemble, tres bien ensemble

Un jour je sais tu comprendras et pour toujours

Que je t'aime ma Michelle

The Beatles/Paul McCartney 1965

That song was so beautiful to me and when I sang it in French, I REALLY butchered the words. So, I sang it over and over and over, especially when I realized if I made mistakes, no one could tell the difference. Anywho, we were only allowed to speak French in class. "Puis-je aller a la salle de bain?" That was me asking to go to the bathroom. Every day, during French class, I went to the bathroom to stall for time. There was too much class participation and I just wanted to take the book home and teach myself. I must admit, it helped to hear her pronounce the words and it was funny to watch her face as she grunted for effect. But an hour was a long time to speak French. I soon realized there was another important reason to take a break at this time. As I rounded the corner, I ran into Mark Brown on his way to detention. Nothing had changed between us. He still gave me butterflies every time I saw him. I realized that now Tammy Hammer was at another school, and I didn't have to hold back my feelings for him. I would later reunite with Tammy in High School, but by then she had gained quite a bit of weight and suffered from severe health problems. I learned her dad, who helped me the day I broke my shoulder died shortly after their move. And sadly, Tammy Hammer would never have the chance to get married or have children. She died from cancer at an early age. Of course, I didn't know that at the time.

I looked forward to seeing Mark every day in between classes. Even though it was only minutes, I would replay every word we spoke and every glance we took in my mind. I loved the way he said my name. I loved the way he smiled like he would burst, just like he did in the sixth grade. Every day as I rounded the corner, he would be there; sometimes waiting. This was the highlight of my day. We would stop and talk about absolutely nothing. Then for two days in a row, he didn't show up. And it hit me, detention was up. My only hope now was to see him at lunch or on the buses. We never had the same classes.

On the third day, I really did have to go to the bathroom. Before I could open my mouth, the French teacher waved her hand at me and said, "aller!" So much for my tale of having a "vessie faible." I ran into the hall and around the corner and smacked right into Mark Brown. He grabbed me as I started to fall and somehow landed on top of me. We both stared into each other's eyes, just like in the Doris Day movies. And then we kissed, and time stood still. Eventually he helped me up and we both just stared at each other. I almost walked back into class and then remembered I had to go to the bathroom. This was not the best time to "pee my pants" so I took off to the bathroom yelling, "bye Mark!" I must have been gone awhile because when I dropped the hall pass off at Ms. Snooty Pant's desk, she stood yakking away in French with her hands on her hips. She waited for my response. "Je ne sais pas," I answered. This means "I don't know" in French- I said it quite a bit- but she was satisfied for now. My love of the French language often paid off. When I went to the Island of St. Martins in the Caribbean as an adult, we were told half the island is French and half the island is Dutch. The Dutch side had a solid grasp of the English language, but the French side-not so much. One day, we went over to the Island of St. Barts and traveled inland to a restaurant for lunch. After lunch, I asked a Frenchman "where is the beach?" or "ou est la plage?" That smartass said, "the beach is all around us." I wanted to say, in French, "you know what I mean, where is the beach access" but I didn't know how. So, I said, "merci beaucoup ane," or "thank you very much jackass." He sneered at me as he tried to figure out if I meant to say this. I am not fluent in French, but I can understand it and speak some French.

The day of my first kiss and later in the day when I was in science class, a "Grove" boy walked into the room, and he came right up to my desk. He handed me a folded note as if he were an Army Private handing an assignment to his Sergeant. I opened it and the note said, "From Mark Brown. To Michelle Martin. Do you want to go with me? Check yes or no." I checked "yes" and handed him back the paper. He looked down at it, smiled and ran off. I sat there in total shock. Mark Brown had never been with any girls before. He was the most popular and best-looking boy in school. All my friends were going to be so surprised. When the bell rang, I gathered my books, and he was waiting for me outside. He took my books, held my hand, and walked me to class. From that day on, he walked me to and from every class, to and from lunch, and to and from the buses. For the first time in my life, I was in love. We did everything together. He would call at night, and we would both leave the phones off the hook so we could pick them up the next morning and tell each other, "Hey wake up, are you there, ok, see you at school." I went to church with his family at Sugar Creek Presbyterian Church. He had an equally gorgeous and popular older brother named "Mitch", but he was never home. Mark and Mitch were total bad asses and all the boys were afraid of them because they could REALLY fight. Mark and I would meet at Eastland Mall and watch ice skating, go to the movies, go to Farrell's ice cream parlor and Annabelle's restaurant. Sometimes I would go to his house, which was huge, and we would "make out" in the basement. He even coordinated his baby blue suit to match my dress when we went to the prom. I felt like Cinderella. I remember Mama Kate used to say, "if you marry in yellow, you will marry a fine fellow, if you marry in blue, your marriage will be true, if you marry in pink, your marriage will sink and if you marry in white, your marriage will be alright." I wasn't getting married, but my love was true.

At Christmas and Thanksgiving, I went to my dad's, and this started a tradition. I went every year after that. At first, we gathered at Mama Gina and Daddy Jim's, later my dad rented out the Fish Camp and as I got older, we went to his ranch. Kerry called my dad's ranch, "The Ponderosa." I still went to Plaza Presbyterian Church every week and now it was even more fun because we had "youth group." Every year, as a group, we would visit Montreat, NC in the Fall and Boone, NC in the winter. I will never forget the solace of the snow in Boone. There was always at least a foot of snow, and we would sled, make snow angels, and have snowball fights. Keep in mind, it hardly ever snowed in Charlotte, NC and when it did, people lost their minds. Everyone headed to the grocery store for bread and milk because, even if you had bread and milk, you needed more. In the South, snow is a big deal. Rule to thumb is, if it snows more than an inch, school is cancelled, and the entire city is shut down.

Spring of that year, after prom, softball practice started, and things started to change with Mark. One day when I got to school, he wasn't waiting for me. He didn't call me to tell me he was sick. I looked for him class after class and he wasn't there. Each time my heart sank. I didn't see him until lunch. I stood waiting for him as he walked up to me. He looked down at the ground and said the words I never expected to hear, "I want to break up." I know I looked shocked and hurt. I can still feel the pain in my heart. We stood in silence as I held back tears. There was nothing else to say. It was over. He turned and walked away. TURN THE PAGE

When I was just a little girl

I asked my mother, what will I be

Will I be pretty? Will I be rich?

Here's what she said to me

Que sera sera

Whatever will be, will be

The future's not ours to see

Que sera sera

When I grew up and fell in love

I asked my sweetheart, what lies ahead

Will we have rainbows, day after day

Here's what my sweetheart said

Que sera sera

Whatever will be, will be

The future's not ours to see,

Que sera sera, what will be, will be

Doris Day

CHAPTER 9 THE CARDINAL RULE

Slowly the Plantation began to come back to life. Mario was back and started taking care of the grounds again. Tim and Amy, my cottage neighbors filled up the chicken coop with new chickens. (There's nothing like roosters crowing in the morning or randomly throughout the day) Alex was still in the cottage by the koi fishpond. The fish were just as beautiful as ever. I fed them and checked on them every day.

As the virus got worse, people learned to adapt to the changes. Anson County is small and rural, but COVID deaths were around forty and increasing every day. In the cottage, my bedroom is a loft that used to be the food storage house for the plantation. It has a movable trap door with a spiral staircase beneath so they could load food, person to person and then close the trap door. In my bedroom, built into the wall, is my bed. I have never seen a bed like this. It is a large human size wood box built into the wall. I put a mattress over it, and it helps my back because it is so firm. Add blankets, a comforter and tons of pillows and viola, it's a comfortable bed. But I learned the hard way, there is a large crack beside the bed just big enough for something to fall through. My tablet fell in there one day and it was history. I was planning to get a new tablet anyway. There was no way to get to it without sawing through the bed and the wall. After that, I stuffed that crack with blankets and was careful about keeping things away from it. And then my new rescue cat Bailey came along. On this day, I had my phone charging on a table. It seemed impossible for her to get that phone down the crack but somehow, she did it. When I started looking for my phone, she was lying in the bed licking her paws and I saw the charger wire underneath her. I was hoping the phone was connected to it and then I heard it ring, from under the bed. She looked at me and I looked at her. I almost screamed. All my photos, SIM card, apps, and the last fifteen years of precious memories were on that phone. I had to get it back.

I ran to the mansion to see who was there and John McNeil was visiting. John McNeil used to be the pharmacist in Norwood and knew my dad. When I tried to explain the situation to him, he didn't understand so we walked over to the cottage so I could show him. He told me he loved my "zoo", and we walked up the stairs. As he pulled the mattress off and looked, he was more than a little shocked. Now things like this happen to me all the time but he looked back at me like this was the craziest thing he had ever seen. He said, "how did you get the phone down that crack?" I told him the cat did it. As he eyed me suspiciously, he dialed my phone number, and it rang under the bed. He said, "I don't like that cat. Let us go look for a skil saw. We're going to have to cut the wall and/or bed out." I nodded my head and wondered what a skil saw was. Then John and I went in search of saws. In the shed, we found about three manual saws which we took but we really needed an electric saw as well, so we decided to drive to the neighbors and borrow one. First, we headed to Lisa Browns', but she wasn't home. I went through her shed and John yelled, "You can't do that." I said, "she'll see me on her deer cam, I waved to her." But I didn't find a saw. He shook his head and said, "Walter Edwards will have one." As we passed Mama Kate's old house, I realized that this used to be "Tootie Edwards" where the Browns "borrowed" the lawnmower to go to church. And sure enough, he had one, so we set off with one fancy electric saw and three hand saws. I could just feel that phone in my hand. The next thing you know we were just sitting on that bed with all the saws. He plugged in the skil saw and commenced to sawing and sawing and sawing. It was a circular saw, so it wasn't fitting exactly right. I pulled out the hand saws and started sawing. I tried each one. Of course, I cut myself, bled everywhere and had an asthma attack but my nebulizer was right there. While I had a breathing treatment, he tried again. After my breathing treatment, he said, "do you have to have this phone?" I told him I did because of the SIM card, and he said, "I hate that cat." Finally, we could see it but did not reach it. I grabbed a hand saw and started sawing like crazy and reached in and grabbed the phone. I thanked John McNeil after walking him back to the Main. We had sweat pouring down our faces, I had blood all over me and we looked like we had been through a tornado. When I walked to the bed, there were wood shavings everywhere, blood splattered on the wall and the mattress was on the floor. Bailey waltzed up the stairs and looked up innocently at me and said, "Meow." I wanted to smack her into next week, but I didn't. The next day as Mario came to see his new project, he said, "how did this happen?" I just pointed to the cat, and he burst out laughing as I told the story.

Christmas was coming up and it just did not feel like Christmas. I didn't even have a tree up. There was no way for anyone to travel and see their family without putting themselves in danger of catching the virus. Suddenly, I felt empty. I prayed and tried to remember the true meaning of Christmas, but it seemed hopeless. Then a secret Santa gave me a generous sum of money for Christmas. He said to "pay it forward" and so I did. I shopped online to spoil my grandchildren and then used video chat to talk to them. Then I put cash in envelopes and left it on people's doors that I knew needed the money. At the store, I paid for the person behind me and that is not easy to do without drawing attention to yourself. I knew God did not want that, but I had to wait for my card. This young woman said she didn't deserve it and started crying. The cashier said, "Yes, you do Honey! It's Christmas and that's the Christmas spirit!" When I walked out, I could feel my heart glowing inside. Then Brandi and I spent Christmas together. We went shopping, out to eat and to Candlelight service at The Red Hill Baptist Church. This ended up being my favorite Christmas of all. After I took Brandi back to her dad's house, I realized how blessed I was.

There was only one more incident, and after that, Bailey had to be spayed. I call it, the "attack of Ladybug Village." The plantation is overflowing with "ladybugs" or "lovebugs." In the main house once, I thought Helena was killing them and I said, "oh no, you can't kill lovebugs!" She wasn't. She was just sweeping up dead ones. I have always considered them special. They are colorful little beetles that eat mites, drink water, love chocolate and can fly. How do I know they love chocolate? Some bored scientist did an experiment and proved, without a doubt, ladybugs love Hershey's chocolate. That makes the next thing I did not seem so silly. The ladybugs are attracted to light and hung out on the lamp by my bed so one day, I made them a village out of index cards and water in a bottle cap for a pool. If this reminds you of Jack Nicholson in "The Shining," the thought did enter my mind, but Mama Kate always did say, "Missy you have quite an imagination." You also must remember, this was during COVID. Anywho, one day all the lady bugs were chillin in the village and out of nowhere, a huge black and white monster leapt onto the village and the village was destroyed. Luckily, no ladybugs were hurt in the disaster, but I decided not to rebuild. It was just too enticing for Bailey.

As I lie in bed, I can look out the circular window on the wall and see what the weather is like, which gives Alexa a break. The trees were bare and one bright red cardinal sat on a branch staring back at me. Bright red cardinals are males, and this one was cute and fat. They are North Carolina's state bird and according to folk lore, when you see one, you are being visited by someone on "the other side." Day after day, in the afternoon I would lay there, and we stared at each other. Then one day, he wasn't there. I got up to look out the window, and a bright red feather was stuck to the window. My heart sank. I put on my gloves and coat and ran outside. There below my window, was a dead cardinal. This was not only a bad omen, but I felt somehow responsible. I picked it up and it was flat from the force of hitting the window. I buried it under leaves so the animals wouldn't disturb it. Then I went back inside. I sat in my new fuzzy round chair and sulked. Did this bird die trying to visit me? What did this mean? I was reading too much into this. Then I looked up and on the refrigerator was a calendar with a cardinal sitting on a bare branch. I said aloud, "Okay God, help me figure this out." I grabbed my phone and called my children to check on them. They were fine and so was Kerry. I got the feeling they were not in any danger. Then it hit me, I was in danger. The warning was for me. I prayed and boldly told God; I have things left to do here. I want to help people, spend time with my children and grandchildren, rescue animals, write and paint, trade stocks and so many other things. Then I gave it to God because I knew I couldn't run from it. The next few days I would be extra careful. A winter storm was coming, and I only needed to go one place and that was the bank. I had to give them a handwritten note requesting a customized statement to start trading stocks. I would have to go tomorrow because the weather would be worse each day. It was my only window of opportunity.

The next day when I set off, I dressed warmly with gloves, a hat, and a coat. I made sure I had my inhalers, epi-pen, and phone. I checked my tires and my gas. I prayed for angels to protect me and my car. Then I drove off as slowly and carefully as I could. It was freezing outside, and it started to sleet. I was only a few miles down the road and as I went around a curve on Randall Road, another car was coming, I hydroplaned, water covered my entire windshield, I hit a pothole and my steering wheel locked up. I braced for some type of impact, but the car rolled to a stop in front of Fred Randall's store. This was the old General Store at the fork in the road in Eggtown where Daddy Jim and I went to get cokes, crackers, and hoop cheese when I was a little girl. Of course, it was closed now. I just sat in shock. I tried to move the steering wheel, but it wouldn't budge. As I sat trying to make sense of what had just happened, I realized I had to get help. I looked down the street at Wendall and Tonya's house. I couldn't make it that far with my asthma. It was too cold outside. I didn't know the people across the street, and it didn't look like they were home anyway. Then I glanced over at Randall Transport. I knew I had to go there but I didn't want to. Randall Transport was owned by Kevin Randall and his parents, (grandson of Fred Randall) and Kevin Randall was my crush. (I later found out he had a girlfriend) I had already run into him several times at church and saw his Mama at the Dollar General. He was going to think I was stalking him. But I didn't have a choice. I made it to the front porch which was covered and knocked softly. I heard voices inside so I knew they would eventually see me. Then I called Robin, and he didn't answer. I called Kerry and told him what happened just as Helen Randall came to the door. I told Kerry I would call him back and hang up. As I explained to Helen what happened, I looked for a mask in my pocketbook. She said to come in and tell her husband, Harvey. Kevin Randall wasn't there. Harvey and I drove over to my car so he could look at it. He couldn't figure it out so he said he would send his cousin Max over in a tow truck. He asked me if I wanted to wait inside and I said, "no, but thank you." Then I called Kerry and asked him to come and pick up this paper and take it to the bank. He said he was on his way. I had the car running for the heat and I kept hearing a "thumping" noise, so I cut off the car and popped the hood. Once again, I prayed, "Lord don't let this be an animal." It wasn't. A belt was hanging down. When Kerry got there, he took the papers and looked at the belt. He pointed to a mark and said, "see this mark- when you hit the pothole and the water splashed up, it knocked your serpentine belt off. The belt is fine. You just need someone to put it back on and I don't have the tools." Then he handed me the belt and left. About that time Helen Randall pulled up. She must have seen Kerry and mistaken him for a serial killer, so she drove over to check on me. That was brave of her, but I told her it was my brother and held up the belt. She drove to her house right down the road and made me some hot chocolate. I drank it and walked back to her office. Cousin Max had called and didn't know how to put the belt on, and she couldn't leave the office to take me home because everyone had left her there alone. So, I called Mario to come and get me. Mario didn't speak English that well and he lived in Stanly County. He had no idea where "Eggtown" and "Two Bucks" were- (that's what people had called Fred Randall's store and the forks of Randall Road) I told him how to get there and after that, I thanked Ms. Helen and headed back to the car. As I held the serpentine belt in my hand and waited for Mario, I felt a sense of relief. When Mario got there, he had put the belt back on in five minutes. Kerry called and said he had delivered the letter for me. As I headed home, I stopped at Mike Lee's store for milk and cat food. I was asking Sherry Ponds about the store's pregnant cat. She said, "well she had her kittens but I'm not sure where." I said, "Well where's the baby daddy?" (the other stray) And about that time 800 walked in the door, heard what I said, twirled around and walked right back out.

When I got back home, I laid down to think about how blessed I was. And there in the round window, I saw the little fat cardinal sitting on his branch.

It was a different cardinal that had hit the window and died. It wasn't my fault. As the cardinal sat transfixed on the window and I stared back, I asked "what is the message?" And the answer was, "you may see a physical death, but I am still with you, watching over you. Always remember the Cardinal Rule. If you are still on this earth, you have a purpose. Find it!" Then he flew away. I walked downstairs to go outside to see if I could find him and when I opened the door, there were cardinals everywhere-in trees, on the bushes, sitting on the fence...they were all around the cottage. Tears filled my eyes. I never saw that cute little fat messenger cardinal again. He had completed his mission from "the other side" and delivered the Cardinal Rule.

Another day has gone.

I am still all alone

How could this be?

You're not here with me?

You never said good-bye

Someone tell me why

Did you have to go?

And leave my world so cold?

Every day I sit and ask myself

How did you slip away

and something whispers in my ear and says

That you are not alone

I am here with you

Though you're far away

I am here to stay

But you are not alone

I am here with you

Though we're far apart

You're always in my heart

But you are not alone

Michael Jackson

CHAPTER 10 IN THE VALLEY

My last year of Junior High School was bittersweet. After going with Mark Brown, I could have any boy I wanted, except the boy I wanted. There were so many good-looking and popular guys that I hung around with- mostly to try and get over Mark. Even though I had many close friends at school, my home life was miserable. As long as I can remember I had suffered from depression. Depression is not just feeling sad. Depression is debilitating. When it hits, it seems permanent. I would force myself to eat. Sleep was an escape. Often, I felt as if I couldn't move but only stare straight ahead. I was stoic and numb to life. The thing that most people don't understand about depression is there is no reason for it. Logically I had every reason to be happy. Instead, I felt as if I were in a deep dark well all alone. Whenever I started to feel this way, I would go to Ansonville to stay with my dad. Being in the country and in nature gave me a sense of peace. By this time, Kerry had already married and divorced at sixteen. He had a son named Jason, so I was an aunt at the age of twelve. On the weekends, my dad would put me in a pasture to bush hog all day and that was fine with me. Having sons on a farm was a big plus, girls were a big minus. I tried to keep up with them, but they had an advantage, they were there all the time. I would rather mow than open and close gates all day. The movement and sound of the mower eased my pain like a baby being rocked in a rocker. I wondered if I was ever rocked because the thought of a human's touch made me uneasy. It wasn't like that with Mark. That's what I missed so much.

My dad would pick me up at the end of the day and take me to the Deluxe Grille to eat. At the time, my dad was my hero. I respected him and I wanted his approval. In fact, I wanted to be just like him. Everyone knew him as a badass cowboy- the best around. There was no doubt that he was the toughest man I had ever known. He may have failed as a father but when it came to being a cowboy, he was the best. My stepfather Richard was a good father figure to Michael and me. He was an amazing man.

Richard was so humble. I wonder if he had any idea what a lifesaver, he was for me, and even Michael. He used to play cards with us and something as simple as that made us feel "normal." Richard suggested that I start babysitting, so I put flyers in everyone's mailbox and the next thing I knew, I was in business. Not only was it fun to babysit but I got paid for it. I would play with the children, get them ready for bed, do my homework and then fall asleep. I started saving my money and Richard helped me open a bank account so I could save money for my first car. I felt sorry for Richard because he had to put up with my mom. She pushed people away and was incapable of love.

I think when you start off in the valley, the reasons you are there are unclear. Over time, exposure to the same dysfunction over and over takes a toll on your mind and eventually your physical body. When people say, "Smile," I want to say, "No, I don't want to." I watched a movie called "Valley of the Dolls" and then read the book.

You've got to climb Mt. Everest to reach the Valley of the Dolls

It's a brutal climb to reach that peak.

which so few have ever seen

You never knew what was really up there.

but the last thing you expected to find was the Valley of the Dolls

You stand there waiting for the rush of exhilaration you thought you'd feel but it never comes.

You're too far away to hear the applause and take your bows.

And there's no place left to climb, you're alone, and the feeling of loneliness is

Overpowering-The air is so thin you can scarcely breathe-

Jaqueline Susann

Valley of the Dolls was about the life of three women: Anne, Neely, and Jennifer. I could relate to each one. I felt like Anne on the inside, Neely on the outside and Jennifer's relationship with her mother mimicked my own relationship with my mother. Ironically, the actors from the movie followed the fate of their characters in real life. Barbara Parkins (Anne) left show business and moved back home. Patti Duke (Neely) suffered from drug addiction and mental illness. And sadly, Sharon Tate (Jennifer) was pregnant when she died shortly after the movie came out. She was infamously murdered by Tex Watson, Susan Atkins, and Patricia Krenwinkel of the Manson cult.

In the movie, Jennifer's mother is only concerned about herself. She sees Jennifer as an extension of her. Image and material means are her mother's top priorities. Mothers with Narcissistic Personality Disorder, like mine, constantly seek attention and have a grandiose sense of importance. These mothers expect perfection out of their daughters and when their daughters succeed, they often get jealous and extremely critical. When the daughter responds with anger, the mother acts as a victim and tries to shame the daughter for treating her so poorly. My mother is loud. She dresses and talks inappropriately. Her clothes are flashy, skimpy and she often tries to coordinate them with her bright blue eye shadow. That's why I never wanted to be in the spotlight. The spotlight could be UG-I-LEE. Sometimes in a store, I would start looking at things on the shelf and pretend like I didn't know her. Once she wore white pants, bled through them, and made sure everyone around knew what happened. I was mortified. Sometimes you forget the exact events or emotional traumas, but you memorize the self-defeating thoughts. One of the worst things she did was involve me prematurely in an adult world. Her life was full of darkness and negativity like the masquerade of an imbecile performing for the world. She used triangulation to manipulate people. She would express her critical thoughts of me to family and friends, hoping the chatter would get back to me. This passive-aggressive behavior fed her fragile ego. Our narcissistic culture reinforced her existence.

When wealth occupies a higher position than wisdom, when notoriety is admired more than dignity, when success is more important than self-respect, the culture itself overvalues "image" and must be regarded as narcissistic.

Alexander Lowen

I always tried to make excuses for my mom and my dad, but the bottom line was my mom was mentally ill, and my dad was greedy. Around this time, I started using drugs and alcohol to escape the nightmare of depression. For the next five years, I would use drugs and alcohol on a regular basis. My best friend at school was Bonnie Carver. She was beautiful and fun loving. We went to parties together and I spent as much time as I could with her. Her giggles made me smile. She was the light I needed in my shadowy world. The first drugs we started doing were "black beauties" or "speed." Speed gave me energy and made me feel great. There were no hangovers, like drinking alcohol. Tina Johnston helped me get my first job at Roll-A-Round skate center and I saved enough money for a 1974 Hunter Green Camero- five speed with my name hand painted on the side. I was the shizit. Bonnie got a black Camero, and we spent our summer at pools, her dad's Country Club and Myrtle Beach.

Myrtle Beach was so different then. There was an amusement park, an area to cruise the strip, a place where Rock bands played, and people stayed up all night and wandered around. Then the next day, they would sleep in the sun all day and then get ready for the clubs. Keep in mind, we had no computers or cell phones. We stopped at phone booths to call people. There was a number you could call to find out what time it was. Our TVs only got four channels and they went off the air at midnight. The Star-Spangled Banner would play and then everything would go fuzzy. We went roller skating on Friday and Saturday nights and since I worked there, I got paid for it. We dialed our landline phones with our fingers and waited for each dial to turn for each number. If we needed a phone number, we looked it up in the phone book. When we wanted to know what was coming on tv, we looked in the TV Guide and then memorized it because the same shows came on the same nights each week. Every Saturday at noon, the white kids watched "American Bandstand" and the black kids watched "Soul Train." I watched both.

When Summer ended, half of the JT William's students went to West Charlotte High School and the rest of us went to Independence High School. Bonnie and I became Patriots along with a thousand other students, including: Tammy Hammer, Caroline Martin, Teresa Farmer, Charlotte Almond, Mark Brown, Sandra Wellman, Tanya Buff and Liz McKenzie.

Where are they now?

Tammy Hammer-deceased, Caroline Martin-still friends, Teresa Farmer-still friends, Charlotte Almond-still friends, Mark Brown-Facebook friends, Sandra Wellman-still friends, Tanya Buff-Facebook friends, Liz McKenzie-moved to Arizona.

We didn't know it at the time but at Independence, we would meet people who would change our lives forever.

Gotta get off gonna get

have to get off from this ride

gotta get hold gonna get

need to get hold of my pride

When did I get where did I

How was I caught in this game

When will I know where will I

How will I think of my name

When did I stop feeling sure feeling safe

And start wondering why wondering why

Is this a dream, am I here where are you

What's in back of the sky, why do we cry

Gotta get off gonna get out of this merry-go-round

gotta get off gonna get need to get on where I'm bound

When did I get where did I: Why am I lost as a lamb

When will I know where will I How will I learn who I am

Is this a dream, am I here, where are you,

Tell me, when will I know how will I know

When will I know why

Dionne Warwick

CHAPTER 11 INDEPENDENCE

It was time for Friday Night Football! Bonnie Carver and I were going to our very first Independence Football game. I still have the picture her mom-Shirley, took of us that night. We were grinning from ear to ear. Bonnie wanted to wear cowboy hats and I did-reluctantly. When we showed up, you would have thought we were movie stars. She knew how to get attention. I really didn't care what happened that night, I just enjoyed being with her. When I felt darkness, she was my light. We met up with Liz McKenzie and some other friends. It was the start of the school year, and we made so many new friends that night.

Christina Cook and Rodney Atwell were two of those new friends. They were both in several of my classes. The following Monday at school, Rodney came up to me in class. He said his older brother, Randy, saw me at the Football game and wanted to go out with me. My first thought was to stall him so I could think of a reason to say "no," so I asked him to bring me a picture of Randy. I thought that would be the end of it. The next day, Rodney came up to me and handed me a picture. When I looked down, I was more than a little surprised. He was very handsome with dark hair and olive skin. He looked like Mark Brown. But Randy Atwell had just graduated from Independence. Why would he want to go out with a freshman? There had to be something wrong with him, but I agreed to meet him. My curiosity got the best of me.

When we met, I couldn't find anything wrong with him. He was just as handsome in person, easy to talk to and very cool. He ended up being my first "real" boyfriend, meaning we had sex. Now I am an adult. I wore his class ring on a chain around my neck. It was about that time that Bonnie started spending a whole lot of time with her neighbor, Scott Fretz. She told me he was the drummer for a local band called "Sugar Creek" that played at the Myrtle Beach Pavilion. I don't know about that.

When I was not at school, working at Roll-A-Round, or babysitting- I was with Randy at his house. His dad was a police officer and never at home. His mom was sweet unless you pissed her off. Even though his dad was a police officer, Randy got into trouble quite a bit. He broke into houses, raced cars and motorcycles, and was addicted to Valiums. He had a GTO and a motorcycle, and he loved them the way I love Cameros. He worked on them all the time because he was a mechanic. There were always things to do to make the engine run better and faster and to make them hotrods. Once Randy even cheated on me with another girl named Melissa. I was crushed, but I forgave him. At night, he would throw rocks at my window and then crawl in. That was when Mama put bars on my windows. After that, he would throw rocks at my window, and I would let him in through the back sliding glass door. Even though he had problems, he was a hard worker and a good person. I was with him a whole year-which in high school's years, is like twenty.

He never went to the skating rink, because he was too old for that, being nineteen and all. Working at Roll-A-Round was the best job ever. Liz McKenzie, Chip Irving, and Tina Johnston worked there with me. We got paid to hang out with friends and skate. Who could forget those shiny colored balls on the ceiling, rhythm skating, the Hokey Pokey, couple's only skate and taking our skates off at the end of the night to "do the hustle" in the middle of the floor. I was hardly ever at home and life was good. I was so busy that I didn't get to visit Ansonville as much. But when I did, the Camero was the perfect car to drive along those familiar winding roads. I would stop in the middle of town and think about the way things used to be.

It started off as a small village of 150 people with a town well and watering trough for the horses. Swollen streams made travel hazardous much of the year. Wildcats and wolves were an early threat. Scott-Irish immigrants started to arrive between 1730 and 1743. Indians called the Uwharrie and Pee Dee Rivers-"Heighwaree." The Yadkin River was known as "Sapona." Before 1730, aboriginal red men-Cheraws and Catawba's-were known for savage fighting. They even fought the Cherokees and ran them back to the mountains. When the English Settlers arrived, the Indians became friendly with the white men, but the white men brought curses-alcohol and smallpox. In 1750, Anson was established as a town. The first Typhoid Fever outbreak didn't hit until 1817 and then again in 1830, along with a measles epidemic. It is funny how my mind could wander back in time, but only in this place. The smell of muscadines and honeysuckle reminded me of Mama Kate telling me story after story. It became etched in my mind forever.

Back at home, life seemed like it couldn't get any better, and then it did. One day, Randy, Rodney and I were driving around. We had to go to Harris Teeter on Albemarle Road to meet their friend to sell him some weed and to smoke a joint with him. I got in the back seat with Rodney, and we waited for this guy to come outside on his break from work. I was taking a toke off the joint when he got in the car. Randy introduced us and he turned around. The first time our eyes met, they locked. He was the most beautiful person I had ever seen. His hair was sandy dark blonde, his eyes were emerald green, and he grinned like Elvis Presley. I smiled back and nodded my head. There are some moments in time that you never forget-some good and some bad. I will never forget the first time I saw Benny Harris.

The First Time Ever I Saw Your Face

The first time ever I saw your face

I thought the sun rose in your eyes

And the moon and stars were the gifts you gave

To the dark and endless skies, my love

To the dark and the endless skies

And the first time ever I kissed your mouth

I felt the earth move in my hand

Like the trembling heart of a captured bird

That was there at my command, my love

That was there at my command, my love

And the first time ever I lay with you

I felt your heart so close to mine

And I knew our joy would fill the earth

And last 'til the end of time, my love

And it would last 'til the end of time

The first time ever I saw your face, your face, your face, your face

Roberta Flack

CHAPTER 12 BLACK SQUIRRELS

I was on my way to the studio when I saw it. On the plantation, the studio used to be a greenhouse. My washer and dryer were broken so while I waited for new ones, I had to use the ones in the studio. There jumping around high atop a pine tree, I spotted something black and silky. As it came down the tree, I saw that it was a black squirrel. I was mesmerized by its beauty. I had never seen one before and didn't know they existed. I later googled them, and it stated that less than 1% of squirrels were black. This magnificent and special squirrel was as amused by me as I was by her. We stared at each other for a minute before she ran back up the tree.

As I reached the studio and opened the door, I almost fell over boxes. These were boxes of pictures I needed to go through. They were being stored at Kerry's house, but he was being evicted so now they were here. Nana and Brandi were not doing well either, but all of this would have to wait. I dreaded going through these boxes and the memories that would resurface. I had about a week or two before I had to get started. My daughter Devin and her children were visiting from Florida and my son, Chase and his daughter were visiting from Asheville NC. Brandi would be there, and I was looking forward to seeing all my children and grandchildren together. I had not seen them in two years. We were all staying in the Main House and there were just enough rooms. I had to pick Brandi up from her dad's so that we could start cleaning and grocery shopping. It worked out that Brandi would have Etta's old room beside Nona's old room which was now an attic. She said, "Why do I have to have the haunted room?" First there was a chair that moved itself. Then the chair that had been in the hall was blocking the large bedroom, which used to be the General's. Then Brandi called me from the other bedroom. The cushion that was tied to a chair in the corner was now thrown in the middle of the floor. We just kept cleaning. That night we stayed in the cottage and Brandi smoked weed and drank excessively. She said once the kids arrived, she would stop, but I knew she would sneak off and do it anyway.

The next morning when we went to the main house, Brandi and I were so excited-we started to dance to the old song "Kung Fu Fighting" and I kicked my leg too high and almost landed on the floor, I knew then it was time to stop. Devin arrived before Chase, with her children: Lily, Primrose, and Terry. Chase came in shortly thereafter with Josie. This was the moment I had waited two years for, and I cherished every minute of my time with them. For the first time in a while, the mansion was full. Every room was taken and the sound of little footsteps running around upstairs echoed throughout the house.

My oldest granddaughter, Lily, is eleven years old, tall, pretty, and smart. She favors my daughter, Devin. Lily moves and talks gracefully and always has her nose in a book reading. Her brother Terry is turning seven years old, athletic and looks like his dad. I call him my "baby Brad Pitt." Primrose is Devin's youngest daughter, and I was there when she was born. When I say, I was there when she was born, I mean Devin almost had her in the parking lot. The nurses were taking their time and I shouted, "Hey, this baby is coming out!" And I was right. It was a very eventful birth. She is now a little bundle of energy that never stops. One day I went upstairs and watched a cartoon with her, which was enlightening. It was called "Baby Boss." Even though things had changed dramatically since I was a child, they still sang "Frere Jacques" which brought back so many memories. This nursery rhyme was about a friar who overslept and is being urged to wake up and sound the bell for the monk's early morning prayers.

Frere Jacques, Frere Jacques

Dormez-vous? Dormez-vous?

Sonnez les martines! Sonnez les martines!

Ding, dang, dong. Ding, dang, dong.

When I was a child in nursery school, we would sing it in French and then English.

Brother John, Brother John

Are you sleeping? Are you sleeping?

Ring the bells for morning! Ring the bells for morning!

Ding, dang, dong. Ding, dang, dong. Unknown

I looked over at Primrose and she was doing flips on the bed. Her curly blond hair was wrapped around her little angelic face. I had heard from Devin that she had a strong, stubborn personality and after watching her, I saw it.

Chase's daughter, Josie, is getting ready to turn eight years old and I would say she has my personality. She is tough, inquisitive, and not afraid to speak her mind. Josie and I went to the cottage to visit the animals. She has a love for animals and nature. Devin's children call me "Mima" (Michelle+Ma), and Josie calls me "Grammy." I walked her around and showed her the garden and the koi pond. She even saw the Black Squirrel which now had little lookalike babies. Once after one of our walks, as we went into the main house, she grabbed my hand and said, "Grammy, it's okay that most people don't live in a castle." Her pure innocence almost brought me to tears.

When my brother Robin and his family came to visit, Chase played the piano in the parlor. This wasn't just any piano. It was a Steinway in immaculate condition and perfectly in tune. There is nothing more relaxing to me than listening to Chase play. It was breathtaking. After Devin served dinner, I couldn't think of a better ending to this week.

For some reason, the night before they left, I dreamed about Mary Bennett, who was the General's first wife. Not only had she lost three children at an early age, but she had come face to face with Sherman's Army at the age of twenty-three. On March 3, 1865, Judson Kilpatrick's Calvary brought terror and destruction to the citizens of Anson County. People were warned ahead of time that they were coming. Men went into hiding, money from the bank was buried and women took cover in their homes. After the Calvary crossed into Anson County, the Pee Dee River began to flood, and the Confederate soldiers were not able to cross and defend their homeland. Before they arrived at the L.D. Bennett Plantation, they raided the James C. Bennett Plantation where Mr. Bennett was shot and killed on his front porch. This home was later used to film the movie "The Color Purple."

Around 3 a.m. the women of the Lemuel Dunn Bennett Planation, heard the trampling of horses. Mary Bennett's younger sister, Charlotte, who was only fifteen at the time was also there with their mother, Mary Dunn. Mary Dunn had a fierce reputation as an experienced equestrian and protector. There were many stories about her bravery. As the Yankees, threatened to break down the door and kill them all, they opened it to dozens of drunk and rowdy soldiers. The soldiers demanded that Charlotte play a tune on the piano and she played "Dixie." For the next two days, they raided the house of food, livestock, and valuables as they terrorized the women.

These three brave women watched as their home was destroyed. After they left, the women walked around surveying what was left and prayed for the end of this madness. That wish came true, but it took years to rebuild, and some people never recovered.

At the time, I wondered why this came to mind and later I realized, it was for inspiration. After my family left, I smiled at the thought of this new memory, but my smile would soon fade. Once again, my world began to unravel. It started with an early morning call from the police and later Concord Hospital. Kerry had been found in the middle of the road in Kannapolis, NC in his underwear. They questioned me about him and advised me that he would be admitted to the hospital. Next Robin called and said Nana was being moved from the nursing home back to the hospital. She had dementia and was refusing to eat and take her medicine. Then my ex-husband Greg called to tell me Brandi was in jail. She just got her fifth DUI. As I sat on my bed, I knew I had to get ready to go to Concord Hospital. I didn't have time for tears, so my body went into motion like a robot.

I didn't break down until I got to Concord and asked what floor my brother was on, and they said "2nd." I asked what unit that was, and they told me it was the Intensive Care Unit. When I got there, they made me sit outside the unit in a rocking chair. I just rocked and cried. It's okay, I knew that many women over the years, just like Mary Bennett, had done the same thing. A nurse eventually came out to get me, I wiped my face with my sleeve and followed her to a little room. She told me Kerry was in a coma and on a ventilator. We exchanged information and concluded he was withdrawing from Fentanyl. When he came into the Emergency Room, he tested negative for drugs, and I knew he was addicted to Opiates. Did he not know that you must be weaned from drugs and alcohol, or the body shuts down and this condition is incompatible with life? After I went to see him, I left to look for his truck and his son, Jason. I found them both. His truck was in the Kannapolis Emergency Room parking lot with the keys locked inside. Over the next few days, I secured the vehicle and reestablished my relationship with my nephew. We had been estranged for years and I had missed him so much.

The only good news was from Greg. Brandi was on a plane to Orange County, California. She was going to rehab at "Hope by the Sea," which I was familiar with from watching the TV show "Intervention". After several days, Kerry came out of the coma and off the ventilator. He had suffered from a mild stroke. My brother Michael called and said Nana was not doing well and was not expected to live much longer, so I shifted my focus to her and headed to the Stanly County Hospital. Just as I had slept in a chair by Kerry's bed, now I slept by her bed. I didn't really sleep, I just closed my eyes and tried to get images out of my head. First, I saw the image of Kerry on the ventilator. He was bone thin, struggling for each breath, and his hands were tied down to keep him from ripping the ventilator out because he couldn't breathe without it. Then I saw an image of mom. Her arms were purple, black, and blue because her veins had collapsed. Her eyes stared out into space, and she didn't speak. Her body was a blob that never moved. Then I saw an image of an old man's mug shot in a newspaper clipping and my eyes shot open. I looked out the window. There was an American flag blowing against the backdrop of a stormy sky. Tears ran down my cheeks as I thought about where I was. I was born on the floor below in room 307, delivered by Dr. McLeod at 12:22 am on January 3, 1965. I was 20 inches long and weighed 7 lbs. 10 oz.

Chase came from Asheville to see Nana for what we thought could be the last time. He cried as she opened her eyes and smiled. She said his name. After that, she was moved back to the nursing home, and we were no longer able to see her because of COVID restrictions. I got to spend a few days with Chase, which was nice. We went by Nana's apartment to see if he wanted anything, went shopping and out to eat. When we came home, I had an asthma attack and we had to use my epi-pen and call an ambulance. Just another day in my life but I am blessed. I am blessed to have an epi-pen to save my life. I am blessed to have such a beautiful son. I am blessed Brandi went to rehab. I am blessed. Kerry eventually came out of the coma and started talking. After Chase left, it was time for me to go to the studio and go through the boxes of pictures.

At first going through the boxes made me smile. There were old report cards and pictures of me and Benny playing in the snow. I read all his letters and cards remembering the moments when he gave them to me. There were pictures of me and my brothers when we were little. We all had black eyes and toy guns. There were pictures of Mama Kate, Mama Gina, Daddy Jim, and my stepfather Richard. I was almost finished organizing when I came to the newspaper clipping and I almost fell backwards. I don't remember walking back to the cottage or sitting down. I just remembering reading the headline again as if for the first time-

"$ 1 MILLION DOLLAR BOND FOR 74-YEAR-OLD ACCUSED OF SEX CRIMES AGAINST MINOR." The article never mentioned Brandi's name to protect her privacy. All the torture she endured flooded back to me as if to slap me across the face. I cried like a baby. How was she supposed to move forward when I had not? Neither of us had worked through the past, so how could we move forward to the future? Now was her chance and I had to do the same. Brandi would end up being my inspiration. She called me from California every day and after thirty days sober, she sounded like a different person. She was happy and whole. Brandi is a free spirit and a beautiful young soul. In a world of gray squirrels, she is my little black squirrel. **TURN THE PAGE**

Cool Change

If there's one thing in my life that's missing

It's the time that I spend alone

Sailing on the cool and bright clear water

There's lots of you friendly people

That are showing me ways to go

And I never want to lose their inspiration

Time for a cool change

I know that's it time for a cool change

And now that my life is so prearranged

I know that it's time for a cool change

I know it may sound selfish

But let me breathe the air

Little River Band

CHAPTER 13 BENNY

I Love you not only for what you are,

but for what I am when I am with you;

I Love You, Benny

When Benny got out of the car, I immediately tried to erase the image of his face from my mind. There was no way I could ever leave Randy for someone else. I loved Randy and nothing would change that. Was it possible to love two people at once? It didn't matter. I would never see him again, or so I thought.

The next day, I was at Randy's house watching him work on his GTO. As I walked around the car, his older brother, Rusty, started to tease me about a nervous habit I have of biting my lips. When Randy finished, he wiped his greasy hands on a rag and said, "hey, remember that guy we saw yesterday-Benny Harris?" I nodded and he continued. "Well, he told me that my girlfriend was hot! He said she is the most beautiful girl he has ever seen. " Randy smiled proudly and my heart must have skipped a beat. On the way home, those words kept replaying over and over in my mind. The more I thought about it, Randy was not always the best boyfriend to me. He had cheated on me. I tried to clear my mind and forget about Benny Harris. But when I got home, mama said, "there's a boy on the phone for you." I said, "Randy?" and she said, "no, another boy." It was Benny Harris. How did he get my phone number? We talked for about thirty minutes, and it was as if I had known him forever. He told me he would see me soon and when I got off the phone, there was a knock on the door. A delivery man had a dozen red roses- and they were for me. I thought they were from Randy, but the card said, "to the most beautiful girl in the world-Benny." Well, that did it. I didn't know how or why but I would have to break up with Randy. My heart could not be in two places at once.

When school started back in my junior year, as I walked up the hill, I heard someone coming up behind me, and it was Benny Harris. He came up beside me and smiled. I said, "Benny, you don't go to this school." He said, "I do now." From that day forward, we were inseparable. He showed up at all my classes and my locker. We spent time together at the smoking patio during break. We both smoked Marlboro Lights in the box. His favorite song was "Turn the Page" by Bob Segar, and even though he was somewhat of a spoiled rich kid, he was not stuck up at all. He lived in a big, beautiful house across from the Country Club. We would go over there to swim and eat lunch and he would say, "put it on dad's tab."

The thing is, he never acted like he was better than other people. He knew everyone and no one was a stranger to him. He wore jeans, t-shirts, button downs and was extremely low key and humble. He had a quality unlike anyone else-he made things happen. When he wanted something, he got it. I was amazed by him, but for some reason he couldn't tell.

First Letter

Michelle,

First, I want you to know that I Love You so much and I think you know that. Sometimes you tell me you love me and sometimes you say that you don't know for sure. What am I supposed to think? I always worry that there is a possibility that you don't. When we are having an enjoyable time and you get things that you want, you love me. If anything doesn't go your way or you don't get what you want, you get mad and say you hate me. I never say that I hate you. Even when we fight, I still love you. I get very discouraged trying to figure out what is going on! If you would just tell me how you feel, things could be wonderful between us. I will always be good to you and take care of you the best that I can. Please tell me you love me! We have a good relationship, although we fight quite a bit. I don't want us to waste our time together arguing. Write me a letter and tell me how you feel. It worries me tremendously when you doubt your love for me. Always remember, I DO LOVE YOU! Benny

One morning mama caught him sleeping in Michael's closet. Benny and mama had an ongoing feud which didn't faze him a bit. He did have a jealous streak, just like I did when it came to him. I didn't want to share him with anyone. I wanted him all to myself. He felt the same. One day he told me he wanted to fight Mark Brown and became obsessed with the idea. They eventually did and afterwards always avoided each other.

Our drug of choice at the time was Quaaludes. You could take a "lude" and it was like drinking a case of beer without the hangover. I didn't drink that much but when I did, I would binge drink. I overdosed and had blackouts several times. Throwing up always saved my life. We went to parties, skipped school, and stayed in trouble. Our hard partying ways and passion for each other was usually a recipe for disaster, especially when I suspected him of cheating.

Second Letter

Michelle,

I am sitting here listening to Segar. I love it. My mom just left. She said I am an alcoholic and dope addict. If she only knew that I'm an angel compared to 65% of the people, our age. She was asking me if I thought you were good for me. I said don't start on Michelle. She is just trying to blame you for everything. We both know that if anything you are a good influence on me. I stopped right here to go and ask her what she did with my Lynyrd Skynyrd Whiskey T shirt, and she said she threw it away. I must get away from here. The only place I can think of is moving to Texas with my cousin, but I can't leave you. I wish you could go with me. I don't know what's gonna happen but this shit ain't working out. If I stay here, I will get sent away to military school. My dad would do that! I wish I were 18 and graduating with you right there beside me so we could start our life together. Whatever happens, I need you to stand beside me always. I wouldn't mind living in Ansonville with your dad. We could live there together. She is standing here watching me write to you. I love you so much and that makes everything harder. I would have been gone months ago but I can't leave you. Here comes my dad, I Love You, Benny

There was one thing about it-Benny loved Ansonville like I did, and we would go there to get away from things. Me, Benny, and Kerry could REALLY get into some trouble together. Benny and Kerry were like two peas in a pod. Kerry was already divorced and wild as a buck. One night in Ansonville, we went looking for a party and saw a Jupe Joint. We heard loud music and decided to check it out. When we walked in the shack, we were the only white people there. It was as if time stood still, and everyone turned around and stared at us. We just started dancing and before you knew it, we were making friends and having the time of our lives. We all had one thing in common. We never saw COLOR; we only saw PEOPLE. Some may not understand that reasoning today, but it means we see people as equals. That night we crashed at someone's house, and I woke up to the song "Open Arms" by Journey playing on a little clock radio. I looked down at Benny sleeping and his hair was curly and wet with sweat.

He looked like an innocent little boy. Suddenly his eyes opened, and he said, "I felt you staring at me." I said, "I'm putting this memory in my mind forever." He said, "yeah right, you won't remember it tomorrow" and he laughed. We lay in each other's arms and fell back to sleep.

When we got back home, I lost my job at Roll-A-Round and went to jail, but it wasn't Benny's fault. There was a girl at work named Debbie and she told the owner that me and Liz McKenzie were letting people in for free. Me and Liz McKenzie were outside putting shaving cream all over her car when the police pulled in and arrested us for vandalism, while we were still in our gold, red and blue uniforms/dresses. When we walked into the jail, guys started shouting, "hey man, we got cheerleaders." Right after that, Benny and I were fighting, and I was driving my car. I got so mad at him that I don't remember anything but hitting a house with my Camero. Neither of us were hurt and no one was in the house either. After that, of course, his parents really did dislike me.

A good memory is when we had a big snowstorm. Benny lived in a neighborhood that was about six miles away. He called and said he was walking over in the snow. A few hours later, he came walking up. We went outside and played in the snow for hours and my mom took pictures. Then we went in and drank hot chocolate. I never wanted that day to end. When it started to get dark, mama said, "Benny, how are you getting home?" He said, "I can't go home. It's snowing too hard. I have to sleep on the couch." And he did.

After that, I got a job waiting tables at Shoney's and making a lot more money. I got a baby blue 1969 Camero. When it was my birthday, Benny was supposed to "house sit" for his neighbors, so he threw me and Mark Nantz a huge Birthday party there and somehow got away with it. When I ran away from home, he found the perfect place for me to stay-down the street from his house-at Chip Irving's house. Chip's mom, Sally, was the best mom ever in my eyes. She even let me drive her BMW. His house was a place where all the kids spent time together. Me and Mark Gardner would stay up all night doing "acid" and watching MTV. Back then, MTV was only Music Videos. Benny and I went to the Prom and had memories that will last forever, but we became infamous for our fighting. We broke up and got back together so many times I lost count.

Third letter

I wanted to write you a letter, but I don't know what to say. I love you so much, but I feel like you are trying to control me. My feelings are so strong but the hold that you have on me is scary. I don't feel like I could ever just walk away from "us." Our relationship is everything to me and I have no life without you. Please write back to me and let me know how you feel. And please, do not get frustrated and angry with me. You know that you are the first girl I have ever been serious with, and I can't be this perfect person that you want me to be. Well, I better get to bed now. I Love you, Benny

P.S. I came up to the field today to watch you play but they told me y'all were cancelled.

Open Arms

Lying beside you, here in the dark

Feeling your heartbeat with mine;

Softly you whisper, you're so sincere

How could our love be so blind?

We sailed on together

We drifted apart

And here you are by my side

So now I come to you with open arms

Nothing to hide, believe what I say

So here I am, with open arms

Hoping you'll see what your love means to me

Open Arms

Journey

Time after time when I ran away from home, I would end up going back. And time after time, Benny and I would break up and get back together. Once during a breakup, I called Benny and asked him to go to church with me that Sunday and he said that he couldn't. So, I called Scott Pace and asked him to go to church with me since Benny and I were officially "on a break." Scott said "yes" and when we got to church, Benny was standing there waiting to surprise me. What a surprise it was. As I sat there in church-in between Scott and Benny-I knew God had a sense of humor. I prayed to God for his forgiveness and for theirs. Benny forgave me and we got back together. Scott Pace never spoke to me again.

Once when Benny was driving, he caught me by surprise. I knew he was most likely bi-polar, and he was having a depressive episode. He was upset because he wasn't just always fighting with me, he was also always fighting with his parents. Slowly as if in slow motion, he said the words I never expected to hear. "One day I'm going to drive until I hit something. I won't hurt anyone else. It's the only way out for me." I was horrified. He didn't mean it. Was he just trying to get attention? How could anyone say that? Why would he leave me? I was careful about my response. I calmly asked him to never say or think about such a thing again. I told him how much I loved him, and I asked him to promise me that he would never do anything like that. He was silent, but I thought to myself, "there is no way he would ever do such a thing." I was wrong. On August 26, 1988, Benny Harris drove his car into the back of a tractor trailer truck. It was stopped at a light on W.T. Harris Blvd. The state trooper said Benny was driving over a hundred miles an hour, and noted there were no skid marks. It was a well-lit area, and no one was around. TURN THE PAGE

I'll Be Missing You

Life ain't always what it seems to be

Words can't express what you mean to me

Even though you're gone we're still a team

In the future can't wait to see

If you open up the gates for me

Reminisce some time, about that day

Try to black it out but it plays again

Can't imagine all the pain I feel

Give anything to hear half your breath

I know you're still here after death

Every step I take every move I make

Every single day every time I pray

I'll be missing you

Thinkin of the day when you went away

What a life to take, what a bond to break

I'll be missing you

It's kinda hard with you not around

Know you're in heaven smiling down

Watching us as we pray for you

Every day we pray for you

Til the day we meet again

In my heart is where I'll keep you friend

Memories give me the strength I need to proceed

Strength I need to believe

My thoughts I just can't define

Wish I could turn back the hands of time

Still can't believe you're gone

Give anything to hear half your breath

I know you're still living life after death

Every step you take every move you make

Every single day every time I pray

I'll be missing you

Thinking of the day when you went away

What a life to take, what a bond to break

I'll Be Missing You

P. Diddy

CHAPTER 14 THE DAY I DIED

What Hurts The Most

I can take the rain on the roof of this empty house

That don't bother me

I can take a few tears now and then, and just let 'em out

I'm not afraid to cry every once and awhile even though

going on with you gone still upsets me

There are days every now and again

I pretend I'm okay

But that's not what gets to me

What hurts the most

was being so close

And having so much to say

And watching you walk away

And never knowing what could've been

And not seeing that love in you

It's what I'm trying to do

It's hard to deal with the pain of losing you

everywhere I go

But I'm doing it

It's hard to force that smile when I see our old friends

And I'm alone

Still harder getting up, getting dressed, living with this regret

But I know if I could do it over

I would trade, give away all the words that I saved in my heart

That I left unspoken

What hurts the most

Is being so close

And having so much to say

And watching you walk away

And never knowing

What could've been

And not seeing that love in you

Is what I was trying to do

Rascal Flatts

We always went to Myrtle Beach for graduation, no matter who was graduating. This year it was our turn. About ten of us had a beach house in Cherry Grove and we had an epic time. So epic, it became legendary. I remember there was: Bonnie, Tina, Liz, Charlotte, Teresa, Kippie and many more. Liz kept bringing the "Garinger boys" over to visit. Bonnie found one of them hiding under her bed. There were beer bongs, parties, endless trips to the Pavilion, and Cruise in-s. One night, after the Pavilion we went to Mother Fletcher's. Somehow, we always all went in together and then got separated. This night was no different. Everyone left to go to another night club, but Tina and I stayed. We were dancing and having a fun time. The next thing I remember is waking up next to Tina in a beach house. There were male lifeguards all around us. They were getting ready to hit the beach, all in various stages of undress. I watched in awe as one tan body after another walked by and then I looked down at Tina. I could not remember anything. Wait! It was coming back to me. We were dancing with a group of lifeguards, and they asked us to come back to their place for a party. I shook Tina and said, "Wake up Tina, we're in heaven!" She was not amused. She dragged me down some stairs and we went looking for her car in the parking lot. There it was and when we got in, she started asking me questions as if I would know. I said, "Tina, I want some beanie weenies in a can." I got a blank stare. If I had a penny for every blank stare I had ever received, I would be rich. As she scolds me about poor choices, she pulls into a grocery store. Those were the best beanie weenies I ever ate. Yes, I got plastic spoons and a coke. I really didn't want that trip to end because I knew when we got home we would have to start our "adult" life. I didn't have a clue what I wanted to do.

I took a career test which stated that I should go into nursing, so I would start nursing school at UNCC in the fall. My dorm was Holshouser and of course, I was on the tenth floor. Even though Independence was a big high school, going to UNCC was a culture shock. I wasn't used to sharing such a small living space with someone else. Once again, I heard God laughing up in heaven when he put me with my roommate, Deb. Deb was my exact opposite in every way possible. She was a big girl with frizzy hair and glasses. This was a time when I was just starting to love Prince's music. I became a lifetime fanatic. Prince Rogers Nelson was a musical genius. I knew all his songs by heart, went to three concerts, and knew everything about him. This wasn't just a phase; I would always love Prince. Having said that, when I walked into the dorm room and saw all the Barry Manilow posters on the wall, I knew this was going to be a long year. After a week of "Copa Cabana," I knew Deb and I would have to have a "come to Jesus' meeting." We needed to set some ground rules. When we got to the one about not having sex in the room if the other person was there-blank stare. Deb told me that she had never had sex before. Now it was my turn to give the blank stare. Not wanting to know more, I informed her that there would not be an issue then. I began to feel a little protective of Deb after that. She wasn't just nerdy; she was naive and innocent. She had led a very sheltered life. I only got really mad at her one time. That was the day I told her Barry Manilow was gay. I might as well have slapped her face. Bless her heart. I eventually took it back and said, "he's probably just saving himself for you." She said, "do you think so?" I said, "NO!"

Another shock to my system was walking everywhere. If you are hungry, walk two miles to the cafeteria. If you want to go to class, walk three miles there and three miles back. Then there were about a hundred people in each class and not only did the professor not take a roll, but he could also care less if you came to class or not. Pass four tests or fail, now go buy your book at the bookstore for $89.95. It wasn't long before I realized two things: I hated nursing, and I needed a job. After the first year, I changed my major to Business Administration and stumbled upon my dream job. At that age, waiting tables at Darryl's Restaurant was the equivalent of working at Roll-A-Round at sixteen. I had experience waiting tables from Shoney's, but this was the big time. In Hollywood, before you become famous, you are waiting tables. I guess that's what this was like because only the coolest and best-looking people got a job at Darryl's. You had to audition for the job and take a class for a week. That's where I met my new besties: Zane-he was my hookup, Kim-my white soul sister and Chris, my gayest friend ever! We were always together. In fact, the next year Kim and I got an apartment together across the street from Darryl's. After closing at night, we went to clubs until 3 am and then the afterparties. I went to classes, worked, and partied. It was fabulous! I was fabulous, and I was out of control. It was a fun time in my life, but parties don't last forever. At least that's what Prince said.

One night I didn't have to work so I spent the night with a boyfriend. He offered me cocaine and that was one drug I had never had before. I stayed away from cocaine and heroin. He talked me into trying "just one line" and I was hooked. The sensation was incredible, but it didn't last long, and I kept wanting more. Before I knew it the sun was coming up and I had to go to work. As soon as I walked outside, I knew I was in trouble. My heart was racing, it felt like my head was spinning and I felt sick to my stomach. I knew I was overdosing but I just kept going and prayed. When I walked into work, I was still praying. There was no way I could get through this, and I was afraid to tell anyone. When I went into the kitchen, I saw all the server trays were put up and I would have to get them down, so I climbed a ladder to reach them. When I got to the top, my body started shaking. I heard a "thud" and realized it was my head hitting the cement. I felt wetness around my head. I drifted up in the air, all the pain was gone, and I felt so peaceful. When I looked down on the concrete floor below, I saw my body in a pool of blood. I was so confused, I started floating from room to room, looking for something but what? I turned and saw a tunnel, but a voice said calmly "NO!" Then I felt pain, there was darkness and voices, and I opened my eyes. Light appeared but it wasn't like the soft light I saw before; it was brutal and harsh. People were staring at me and calling my name. Paramedics lifted me onto a stretcher. The lights were so bright. I can't remember much about the ride in the ambulance or doctors stitching up my head, but I realized that I had died and come back. Mama Kate had told me that some people were born with a "veil" and had a connection to the spirit world. After that day, I had a veil. I knew things. I saw things. As excited as I was to be able to talk to God and spirits, I learned not to talk about it. People couldn't comprehend what I was saying. The good thing is, I never did a street drug again, and I never missed them. **TURN THE PAGE**

Over the Mountain

Over the mountain, take me across the sky

Something in my vision, something deep inside

Where did I wander, where do you think I wandered to

I've seen life's astral plane I traveled through

I heard them tell me that this land of dreams was now

I told them I had ridden shooting stars

And said I'd show them how

Over and over, always tried to get away

Living in a daydream, only place I had to stay

Fever or breakout burning in me miles wide

I heard them tell me that this land of dreams was now

I told them I had ridden shooting stars

And said I'd show them how

Don't need no astrology, it's inside of you and me

You don't need a ticket to fly with me, I'm free, yeah

Ozzy Osborne

CHAPTER 15 MAMA DON'T LEAVE ME

When Mama was in a nursing home dying from dementia, I put a picture beside her bedside. It was a picture of her as a little girl with pigtails, standing in between Mama Kate and Daddy Paul. She had her arms around them and was grinning from ear to ear. Now, when I glance over at her, I don't see an elderly woman starving herself. I don't see a narcissist. I see a little girl that will soon be reunited with her mama and daddy, and my heart melts. On the day that I got the call, I went to see her one last time. When I got there, I sat by her bed and cried. I was rocking back and forth and saying, "Mama, Don't Leave Me." As I closed my eyes, I was a little girl again hiding in a closet. It was dark, I was holding Michael as a baby and rocking back and forth. I was crying, "Mama Don't Leave Me." That's why Michael never cried, or God and his angels were with us. I felt a hand on my shoulder, and I opened my eyes. A nurse had come in to comfort me. I have met so many horrific nurses but the good ones more than make up for the bad. That day, that nurse, was my angel. I felt mama's cold hands. She was really gone. Mama always wanted her story told, so when I found her journal, I decided to tell it-word for word.

The year 1963 I went to work in the office of George Smart as secretary-bookkeeper. I got to be with people I liked and see my children at school. This was at part-time work, I had just enough time to be at home with my household duties and then be away enough to feel like something more than just a homemaker. I love to be around lots of people, and this was my job in the school, also helping teachers and students. I especially love children and I could see my own progressing well and participating in activities. George and I always talked very much to each other. He was attracted to me long before I went to work for him, but I was not aware of it until I went to work for him. I directed our church choir for a year, and he was in our choir but was always so busy I just ignored any thoughts or ideas that came to my mind. He loved music and that's another thing we had in common.

As we talked at school in between work he would sympathize with any family problem I would have, and I also came to listen to any of his family problems. Just talking was something I always wanted Buddy to do, but he never had time or even better he thought my ideas were stupid.

We began to get closer and closer that year always wanting an excuse to meet each other somewhere when I had to go to Wadesboro shopping. (or Norwood or Albemarle). The times were few the first year and sex didn't play a part in our meeting. We just enjoyed each other's company. That following summer I did not see him but once during the summer. I was pregnant with Michelle, I worked until October of 1964 at the school and Michelle was born January 3, 1965. During the time I was pregnant I did not see George except at church. In March, I went back to work at school, but things were a little different. We had decided that our relationship was going to stop and during the next year, we just met on occasion to just talk things over and say that we loved each other deeply but with our families it was impossible to do anything about it and how wonderful it would have been if we had met before we were married. I had less time to go places than with a small baby and three boys, so things slacked up.

On February 1, 1967, I knew we could not get by with our feelings forever, and the only way we all had any chance was to quit work and not be around George so on that day, I told him I would not be back, and I wasn't. I did not see him at all, I mean even in a public place for two months. We tried to keep away from each other and see how we could get along.

Finally, one-night late George called just asking how I was, and we just talked as any friends would. Buddy never stayed home at night, he always said he had to work all day and then late every night. Mostly he would stay in the store with a crowd of young boys and play cards, or that's what he told me. I used to beg him to stay home with me at night and at least be with our children and I to put them to bed, but not never. Later I began not to even care if he was home or not. We would argue, mostly about money. I wondered why if he worked day and night why he didn't ever have any money. If I asked him for money to buy something for the children or the house or myself, he would say wait until later, yet everyone in our town thought he had money, and I never got the benefit of any from him. This was the main reason I wanted to work so I could have my own spending money. That's when I started my own charge account which he never found out about. This was the only way I would be able to get the children and I things we needed at the time. I'm still paying on that same charge account.

Well, anyway George made a habit of calling me about eleven o'clock lots of nights. He knew Buddy was not at home and our party line would usually be in bed. We got the need for each other more; it seemed like we could never get each other off our mind.

(During this time is when I felt I could have gotten pregnant by George. We were so close, and I knew I could lean on George or depend on him. All I know was how much George meant to me as a man to love me and take care of me. He would always take up for me and I could go to him in any need I had.)

All I could think of was how ugly Buddy had been to me during our marriage, how he had beaten me in front of one of our friends and how he often came home mad and would tear up things I had made for the house, he called it junk. On several occasions, even during any of my pregnancy, he would fight me as he did anytime. Once he drug me across the kitchen by my hair and squeezed my face and throat or kicked me in the stomach with cowboy boots. If ever he got mad, he was very cruel. The children noticed he did not love or respect me; they even told me things at school about how we would fight. This hurt me very deeply because I was very ashamed for people to know just how badly he treated me. People did know that he talked to me ugly in public or would cut some ugly remark about me in front of someone else, but they were not aware he would beat on me, because he did not drink. Just had a terrible temper.

This was the difference George was always so warm and understanding, and patient. He knew what I had to live with. He loved the craft things I made. I would take things to school, and he appreciated my creative ability which Buddy thought was foolish.

On August 8 we had another debate, George, Cora Lee, and me. I was being pressured every way. We met at the baseball field and discussed the problem but came up with no solution. So, during the talk I left and felt if I could get away from all of it, I could have time to think. No one knew I took Michelle and some clothes, and we came to Charlotte. We got a motel room at Travel-lodge under my name. I was there one day and two nights. My mind was in great turmoil about what I needed to do. I could not live under the strain of all the talk and accusations. I talked with George on the phone for a long time and told him not to worry about me.)

On July 25 George and I were caught talking on the phone at about eleven o'clock by his wife at my neighbors. He was on the school phone talking to me and the school was across the street from our house and their house on the other side of the school. His wife suspecting, he was talking to someone and was suspicious of me because she knew he liked me very much. We weren't saying anything to be ashamed of but when we heard the phone click, I said we had better hang up and say good-bye.

Minutes later, Buddy came home mad as fire accusing me and George's wife came and wanted to know what we were up to. She had called Buddy. He and I got into the car to find George who had left the school. He wanted to talk to George and find out why he was talking to me, when we couldn't find him, Buddy drove through town swerving the car, dodging a gas station gas pump. He turned a U turn up the road and as slowing down he had already said he was going to kill us and I felt it so during the turn, I opened the door and fell out on the road. He stopped; this scared him enough to put me back into the car. He then drove me home and carried me into the house. I couldn't walk for a week because of soreness and my knee was knocked out of joint. He went to get my mother. She helped me that week.

Buddy spread the word that George and I were having an affair. I had not told him anything at this time, but he accused me. The next weeks he was the best to me as far as giving himself time, attention, money and making plans for us to go to the mountains for the weekend. We went to the nicest places, and I enjoyed myself except Buddy kept making remarks about me being so cold and not enjoying being with him. But I was pregnant and couldn't tell him. He went out of his way to do things I liked to do. I'll never forget how he had changed, and I wondered if seeing George had caused him to act this way. I should have met George earlier. He would have appreciated me during the first years of our marriage. He was accused of going with a girl when we had been married for two years. He had pictures of her in his billfold and did not carry one of me and I always resented that. I know there was something between them at that time I cared but as the children were born, I got to where I just didn't care. It was too much trouble to worry about it.

The next few weeks he would slip home in hopes to catch me on the phone to George. George still would call me anytime, taking chances just to find out how I was and to tell me how dearly he loved me and how much he missed me. I took several chances to meet him because we had things to tell each other about the strain we were in. We grew increasingly on each other's mind.

I would walk into the house anytime and Buddy would be hiding somewhere in the closet or drive the car home with the lights off or burst into the house. He was making a nervous wreck of me always accusing, scaring, and tormenting me. He would just drill me every day, where I had been, had George called, or just questioning to find out my thoughts about the situation, anything to get me twisted in my words. He got me puzzled and confused as to what I should say. He really knew how to mix up so I would let him know how I felt. If nothing else, he would mix me up in anger, then I wouldn't care about the fact of telling him what I thought. I had George's child. On September 15, he and I went to the doctor together for my pre-natal exam and he had an ailment. I don't remember what it was now. The afternoon we got home somehow George called to find out how I was. In turn Buddy slipped into the house catching us on the phone. Buddy asks George to please leave me alone and he would take care of me. He hung up the phone or took the phone apart somehow, so it did not work anymore.

He and I started arguing. I began to get mad also. He brought up the fact that he could have had an affair with a girl Martha Lowder from Albemarle, if he wanted to. That she seemed to care for him. But he didn't choose to. She worked at the stockyard where he worked several years prior to this event. He said he always had deep feelings for her. In my anger and desperation, I wanted to tell him something because he had hurt my pride years ago by going with a girl Glenda Turner and now this, so being very outspoken and not realizing upon what calamity it would bring I told him that the baby I was going to have was George Smarts' and I had been a wife to him. That he had treated me with love and respect, something he had failed to give me. And that I wanted to leave with George and let him find a place for Michelle to stay. I also told him Michelle was George's mainly because I knew Buddy loved her dearly -this way he wouldn't love her so much and I would get to keep her. I told him she was my life, and I could not stand to leave her. She was smaller than the boys' and had to have a mother's care. The boys were so attached to their daddy, and they thought what he did was wonderful. I didn't feel under the circumstances I could manage the boys on my own. I didn't want to be selfish by tearing them out of their home and school overnight. I had just had enough and was ready to get out of this situation one way or another.

Buddy directly goes to the phone, calls his lawyers. He asks him if he could get me to sign for adultery then if he could get his divorce in one month's time. His lawyer discouraged that and asked for him to come down on Saturday morning. Meanwhile, we got Cora Lee and George to come over to our house. I said I had to leave; I couldn't stand it anymore. I wanted George to take me somewhere. He said he would. He took Cora Lee home, brought his car to our house and I filled it with mine and Michelle's clothes. Before this Buddy gets on the phone and calls three more well known and particularly good men of the town and tells them of all the trouble and he wants to get George fired from teaching the next week. Later he was called before the school board. He just claimed he was a very good friend to me and that there was never anything ugly to our relationship. We felt this was true. He said I was one of the nicest women he had ever met, and he highly respected me.

George and I took Michelle and left that night. I told Buddy I would be back the next day, Saturday, to do something about the situation. George did his best to calm me down, I was hysterical, and I didn't know then what I needed to do but get away from the whole mess. George talked to me, trying to explain we could not leave together and there was no way for me to leave now that he would lose his job for sure and the only practical thing for me to do would be to go home. It hurt my pride if there was any pride left, but he took me back at 12:30. Michelle was not asleep and we took all my things back into the house, it was dark, but Buddy got up and let me in and we talked. He was going to let me come back. There was not much sleep that night because of tears and thoughts raging through my mind.

On Saturday, I got up as usual, cleaned the house, felt a great relief, and seemed happy because Buddy had seemed that morning to accept me back and that made me feel he loved me. He came home during the day and seemed more loving than ever before. On Sunday, we, as a family, seemed happy because we were back together again. I fixed a good dinner and that afternoon we all took a ride to Rockingham; we had thought about going to a movie but decided not to. We then drove to the Holiday Inn and had supper. All the children were with us, nothing was said about anything. He treated me just like a queen. I guess he knew it would be the last.

That night we got home and were getting ready for bed. Sadie Phillips called and asked Buddy if he would take her to her daughter Ann's house because Ann and Tom, her husband, were having a fight and Tom was beating everybody. Buddy did and when he came back, he had Ann with him and her mother and brother and his wife. He let her mother out at her house and Ann, Tommy, her brother, and Dianne, her sister-in-law came to our house, they said to get calmed down. Buddy made several remarks that he would never beat me again, that he had seen what it would do to someone.

Tommy was going to work with Buddy at Laurel Hill stockyard the next week. He begged me to go with them on Monday and I could go shopping, he would give me extra money. I had some housework that I needed to have done but thought to make him happy I would go. Before Ann, Tommy and Dianne left he asked them if they would like to go shopping in Lumberton and of course, they said yes.

The next day the children went to school. Michelle went to stay with my mother, and we spent all day shopping and Buddy working, at lunch we went to pick up Buddy and Tommy. We went to the nicer motel-restaurant for lunch. That afternoon he loved me and acted like he hated so very much for me to leave him and come home. But I had to be there before school was out. I talked to the girls on the way back, they also found out that Buddy and I had lots of trouble, and I made a remark to them that I thought the world of George and would always respect him because he had treated me with the greatest respect.

I did not hear from Buddy that Monday night but on Tuesday or Wednesday he came home and got a change of clothes. He was a completely different person. He took a bath, got his clothes, made a remark that he would never love me again after Monday night and the feeling of my coldness. He was very modest and would not dress in front of me. He left and returned on Friday, changed clothes, took a bath and in his madness undone the telephone again. (I had fixed it back from the last time) He told me I was going to have to do something. He had the telephone out and the car that weekend and he was gone. His mother and daddy and he went to the races in Lexington, Ann I found out later.

He came home Monday morning for clothes, he was going to Norwood stockyard sales that week, but he was gone all week except to get clothes changed and a bath on the next Friday. During that week he threatened me to stay out of the store. I walked down to the store to get a break and milk. He told me he would kill me if I went back to his store. I sent the children down there to get enough food for them to eat. The next weekend he took Ann to Charlotte to the fair and it was our anniversary, September 30th. He didn't show up at all during the weekend, on Monday he came by the house. Mother was there. She heard him yelling at me and he was ready to jump on me again. He said I had to get out of that house so he and the children would have somewhere to live and if I tried to take anything he had, he would kill me and George. He accused me of more of all kinds of ugly things.

He came back on Wednesday and told me we would have to get separation papers and that I would have to go to mother's and live. During that week he had the boys go from school to the store to go home with his mother. He wouldn't let them stay with me yet, he was seeing Ann and living with her, at her brother-in-law's apartment. Everyone in town knows this. I agreed to go on Friday October 7 to sign separation papers. I told him I would go live with mother for a while but that I could not for long. She and I have never been able to get along and he knows that. But that made him happy.

On October 7, 1967, I went with him to Wadesboro to sign separation papers only. This lawyer discussed this with us and gave the facts of what I had told Buddy. After living like I had for three weeks I was even more willing to get away from this. He told me how hard it would be to get out on my own and I told him I knew it, but Buddy had always made me feel that I didn't ever own anything so why shouldn't I have anything now. He wanted me to really feel guilty that I didn't deserve anything. I also stated that I came down just to sign separation papers and that was all. He said everything had to be done that day. With no one to give advice or guidance of legal law, I thought he was telling the truth.

At this point after about an hour I didn't care at the time for anything because he had never been led to believe anything of his was mine and being ignorant of the fact and scared because I had been threatened if I didn't sign them. I didn't think about anything, just whatever they suggested, I okayed it. I came back later to sign the papers. I was so worn out; I went to mother's and went to sleep and told her I wanted to move Michelle and I there the next day. He left and came back on Saturday for me to move in the car. I left the house with all the furnishings except personal clothes, all that junk as he called it, flower arrangements, sewing machine, mixer, etc. Everything else I left in place for the boys as it was for them. Also, a stereo that was given to me was left there. I had no way to get it moved. I left on Saturday; on Sunday I went back over there to take the boys some blankets. The boys were there with a sixteen-year-old boy. Buddy was off with Ann Duke in public, there was no hiding. On Monday I called the boys to see how they were. Ann was there cooking supper. Her children were with her husband, she had just gotten separation papers on Thursday. First Buddy asked me to go on Thursday and then changed it to Friday. Ann and Tom went on Thursday, but I did not know this. Ann took over the 1967 Buick I drove and my house that first week. My mother-in-law did everything she could to get the two together. They are a match. She brought clothes for Ann and treated her like a queen. She has never had anything until this, she is really fixed. Buddy had Johnny, a sixteen-year-old to stay with my boys while he and Ann went and did as they pleased. Johnny's mother has had seven children, and none have the same father. He has brought himself up. He also fell into a good home to get to stay there. He has been father and mother to my boys, what little that is. No one in town could stop this and everyone talked about it.

About a month later, I went to the house to see Kerry, my eight-year-old, he was there sick and by himself. I called the store for Buddy. I wanted him to let Kerry go to mother's and let me take care of him, but he would not. I went back that afternoon, they saw me drive up but they-all children,

Buddy, and his daddy jumped into the car and went to his mothers. I wanted to find out how Kerry was, so I followed them out there. Buddy drove fast then put on brakes quickly so I would almost run over them. I got out of the car at Buddy's daddies, and he told me to get out of his yard, that I didn't have any business there. I told him if they had stopped when they saw me coming, I wouldn't have gone there. They would not even let the children talk to me. <Journal ends>

Ironically, the same Travel-lodge in Charlotte where Mama went for a week was where the church paid for me, her, and Michael to stay when we were hiding from George. He drank, did drugs, was violent, had a gun and put his fist through the wall. He later admitted that he planned to kill her. He had his gun and was watching our house in Charlotte. He was crouched outside looking in through the big front window. As he stood outside and peered in the window, he saw Mama peacefully reading a book. He decided to let her live. He never had anything to do with Michael, even though Michael looked just like him. He was the reason I had to hide with Michael in the closet at night. **TURN THE PAGE**

CHAPTER 16 MONSTERS AND MIRACLES

Purple Rain

I never meant to cause you any sorrow

I never meant to cause you any pain

I only wanted one time to see you laughing

I only want to see you laughing in the Purple Rain

Purple Rain, Purple Rain, Purple Rain, Purple Rain, Purple Rain

PRINCE

When I noticed him, I thought he was smart, good looking, and charming. He worked at Darryl's Restaurant and went to the University of North Carolina at Charlotte. At first, I never saw any signs that there was something wrong with him. When I got pregnant, he wanted me to get an abortion, and so did my mom. I refused. He left and had no contact with me for two weeks, meanwhile I tried to plan my life as a single mother. I got out the phone book and started making calls for assistance. After the semester ended, I would have to quit school and work full time. By this time, Mom and Richard were separated. He lived at a condominium on Old Lantern Way. Kim and I would have to give up our apartment and Richard agreed to let me move in with him. Then after two weeks of silence, he called non-stop. I yanked the phone cord out of the wall. But Ted pulled me aside at work and pledged to take care of me and the baby. He said that he wanted us to be together and we got married. Richard eventually moved into his daughter's guest house and Ted moved into the condominium. It was then that he dropped the act. Once I was dependent on him, it took a few weeks for me to realize I was living with a sociopath. At this point I was getting too big to fight back and I had to protect the baby at all costs. I could feel her moving inside of me and I had never felt a love like this before. I would feel better once she was born and I could physically defend myself. When I was five months pregnant, I got pneumonia and was very sick. I couldn't breathe and begged him to take me to the hospital, but he refused. I called an ambulance and once I got to the hospital, I was admitted to the Intensive Care Unit. I felt safe in the hospital and didn't want to leave. The baby was fine. His mother Lois, brother Doug and my mom were my support system, and I was glad to have them. He mentioned that we should go live with his mother and brother when I got out of the hospital, and I agreed. I knew they would protect me, and they did. Ted was verbally abusive to me and his mom, Lois- but his brother Doug protected us. Doug, Lois, and my mom were extremely excited about the baby. Ted seemed unaware we were going to have a child. He was always too busy or never there, which was fine by me. I finished that school year and worked at Darryl's right up until I had the baby. Her name was Devin Raquel Hudson, and she was the most beautiful sight I had ever seen. I breast fed her and once I got her home, we never left the house. My mom got me a Dr. Spock book and I read it front to back. I consulted this book on everything so she would be a happy and healthy baby. I rocked her and sang to her. I even had a baby calendar where I wrote something different about her every day. Lois, Doug, and I were "over the moon." Ted ignored her. Whenever Ted came in and started raising his voice, I would close the bedroom door and I tried to keep her away from him as much as possible. If Doug wasn't there and he hit me, I would fight him back like a wild cat. I busted lamps over his head, threw things and called the police. He would apologize and say he would never do it again. Sometimes, he wouldn't seem to remember anything that had happened. He was a psychology major and tried his best to "get in my head" and make me think I was crazy. Lois said that I was going to have to learn to put up with his abuse and ignore it. I told her that would never happen. At this time in my life, I focused on Devin. According to Dr. Spock, she was a "colicky" baby which meant she would have stomach cramping. She cried all the time. Mom and Lois said I would have to let her cry, but I couldn't. I would turn on the vacuum cleaner, put her in a basket on the dryer or take her for a ride around the block in her car seat. Dr. Spock was right, all these things worked as long as you didn't stop. I was exhausted. One night I had a glass of wine and breast fed her. She was unusually quiet and wouldn't wake up. I took her to the hospital. The doctor said I had to remember to be careful, everything I ate was going to her. She would be okay but was drunk. When I went to look for this chapter in Dr. Spock's book, it wasn't there. I felt like a failure and a terrible mother. Pretty soon, I will have to wean her so I can go back to work, and she will have to go to day care. I cried at the thought of leaving her.

I knew we wouldn't be able to stay with his mom forever, so I got my first full time job at Ford Motor Credit as a credit investigator. The interaction with other people was good for me and Devin got used to the routine of day care. Ted found us an apartment and started working as a painting contractor, or so he said. He never told the truth and I'm not sure he knew the truth. He was sinister and living in this apartment is when the worst of the abuse really began. I had no idea just how awful things would get. The only good thing was that he began to care about Devin or so it seemed. Only later would I realize he saw us as possessions. I wasn't afraid for her anymore because she was of value to him now, but I didn't know if that would last. I had to stay alive so I could protect her. Every day and every thought was survival. He told me if I left, he would kill me, and I knew he would. It was as if he were the devil himself. His eyes would turn black, and his constant rage was inevitable. I thought about ways to escape but he was always watching me. No one at work knew. I hid all of it with a smile and arduous work.

I noticed a pattern with Ted. First, he was always high on drugs. I suspected marijuana and cocaine. He would stay away for lengthy periods of time, especially at night. He would say he was working and since he was self-employed, I could not keep track of him. I was not allowed to talk to him about money or his business. With him it was either feast or famine, but I never saw any of his money. He would occasionally buy something extravagant for himself. He had expensive taste and where we lived was expensive. I begged him to help me with the rent and if it got too far behind, he would-as if he were doing me a favor. He lived like a king and made sure Devin was provided for, while some nights I went to bed hungry. At 5'6, I weighed 120 pounds, and he told me to go on a diet. Meanwhile, I saw myself as too skinny and I wanted to gain weight. His delusional thinking built up so much anger inside me. When I was around him, I was like a robot. When he left, I spent time with Devin and could relax.

When I tried to follow his "plans," he would change them leaving me perplexed. One day, he said he wanted to move to Columbia, (not South Carolina, the country) then the next day he wouldn't even remember saying it. One night he came and woke me up. He said to take the next day off work and pack because we were moving. He tried to drag me out of bed and told me to start packing. I started throwing things and hit him in the face with a weightlifting dumbbell. He slammed me into a wall and luckily the neighbors called 911. Whenever the police officers were involved, it would save me for one night. Filing charges against him would have been a death sentence. This plan of his to move did take place. We moved to a beautiful ranch styled brick house in Matthews, NC. I had no idea what he had done to get the house and really didn't care because I no longer had to make rent payments. I knew he was doing something illegal, and I hoped he would get caught and go to prison.

It seemed like he never slept but sometimes I would wake up to feel his hands around my throat. Sex with him was a violent rape. Every day was a living hell. Work and alone time with Devin kept me going. At work, my supervisor started having an affair with a colleague. I went to the President of that office and complained. He told me to keep my mouth shut and I gave my two weeks' notice. I went to work at Volvo Finance. Instead of driving a new Ford Probe, I was now driving a Volvo 850. There was one thing about it, I always had an excellent job. It seemed on the outside like I had it all. I started to overspend and run up credit cards. Shopping was an escape for me. I bought clothes, shoes, purses, and things for Devin. On my first day of work at Volvo, I put in a call to Ford's home office and let them know about the affair. She resigned, denied it, got pregnant by him, and later married him. The president of that office retired early. Being tortured at home was starting to make me strong. In fact, I was fierce. I wasn't afraid of anything except him. Slowly over time, I began to work on my exit plan. I would get away from him, even if I had to kill him.

First it started with money. When he passed out, I would go through his clothes and find wads of money. I would take some of it and he didn't seem to notice. Second, I tried to gather as much information as I could about what he was doing. I knew knowledge was power. I found out that he was dealing drugs, and he was involved in some type of mortgage fraud. A big con artist in Charlotte by the name of Eric, was running a mortgage fraud business and this is how we got the house. Eric tried to swindle Ted, but he had met his match. Ted ended up taking the property from him and they went into business together. Ted "owned" another house close by and was leading a double life there. I broke up his "love nest" one night when I threw a chair through the sliding glass door. I was getting stronger and stronger. Then I got pregnant again. I was so happy about it, I put my plans on hold. He stopped seeing the "Hooters girl" but I knew there would always be more. Just as before, he didn't seem to "acknowledge" the pregnancy. I had two miscarriages but this time I made it to six months, so I felt safe. I wanted children so bad. It would be great to have a boy. One day I didn't feel good and stayed home from work. I was watching TV when blood started to seep through my pants. I called my mom, and she took me to the hospital. When things are bad, I try to block them out. I remember having D&C surgery and going home with an empty belly. Ted never came to the hospital. I mourned but not for long. I kept pushing all my feelings deep inside, but it was starting to get crowded in there. I made an appointment with a psychiatrist. He was across the street from my job, and I went there during my lunch break. He diagnosed me with depression and obsessive-compulsive disorder. That's when I started taking Prozac. After a few weeks, I could tell the difference. For the first time in my life, I felt "normal" and not sad. I got pregnant again and had my son, Chase. I called him "baby chase" and he was so beautiful. I couldn't stop staring at him. I concentrated on my children and once again, began to plan my escape. My children were everything to me, unfortunately Ted realized this and began to use them as pawns. For the time being, I had to agree with everything he said and "pretend" to be happy with him.

One night he came in late, and I was up feeding Chase. Ted had blood all over him, especially around his head. He said that he had gotten into a fight, but there was too much blood. Before they caught Ted Bundy, I had considered the fact that it could be him. He drove a Volkswagen, and every detail the police officers covered just fit, but most of the killings were in the west. Ted bragged about killing people. That night I was convinced he was a serial killer. He twisted things around and tried to make me seem crazy. When my friend from work, Janelle, came to stay with us for a few days, I felt safe. She was young and needed some time away from her parents. After two days she pulled me aside and said she was going back home. She said, "Michelle, you have to get out of here. You and the children are in danger. Can't you see that?" I told her that he threatened to kill us if I left. I will never forget her words, "He's going to kill you anyway. Get out!" I talked to my psychiatrist about it, and he agreed. He said I didn't have any more time. Week after week went by and I was afraid to leave, afraid to stay, yet I knew they were right. My time was up. What happened next wasn't planned. God intervened.

One day after work, I picked up the kids from day care and when I came home, he was watching TV. I was surprised to see him but did not say anything. I put Chase in a playpen in his room and had Devin in there to watch him. She was always "my little helper." I told them that I would fix dinner while they played and watched tv. Then I shut the door. I knew they were safe. After they ate, I would give them a bath and get them ready for bed. As I fixed dinner, Ted never said a word. He kept staring at the TV. I took him a drink and a plate of food on a TV tray. He ate, drank, and set his TV tray aside for me to take. As I finished cleaning the kitchen, I turned on the dishwasher. He leapt from the couch, picked me up and slammed me onto the ground. I never saw it coming. He started to beat me and then choked me, and I started to pass out. As I was losing consciousness, I prayed to God. I promised him that if he let me live through this, I would leave the next day and I did.

When I came to, I felt wet, sticky blood in my hair and around my head. Blood was coming from my nose and ears. There was a knot on my head, but I was alive. As I stood up, I felt dizzy. He was back on the couch in front of the TV, but he was shouting. Apparently when I turned on the dishwasher, the noise made him miss something important on TV. I quietly cleaned myself and the blood on the floor, then I went to take care of the children-never uttering a word. When he left the next morning, I would pack up as much as I could and go to my mother's house. After putting the children to bed, I just crawled into bed and did not move. I prayed over and over as tears ran down my face. When I opened my eyes, he was standing in the doorway. He said, "sleep well, it may be your last. You may not make it through the night." But I did. **TURN THE PAGE**

CHAPTER 17 BECOMING AN EAGLE

Eagles rise above the storm. They are strong, powerful birds that can see well into the distance. The wind of the storm pushes them higher and higher. I knew it was time for me to become an eagle. Ever since my "Near Death Experience," I had felt a spiritual connection to God, angels, and souls on "the other side." I decided to live day to day and not worry about the "what ifs." I gave all my worries to God that day and waited for him to lead me.

I called in sick to work and my brothers helped me move clothes to my mom's house. The kids went to day care and when I picked them up, we went to stay with my mom. I knew he would take them from day care the next day but there was no way to run from him. For one thing, I didn't have the resources. For another, I would always be looking over my shoulder. It was time to face my fears. I pictured giant angels all around us.

Even though I knew he would take them, when he did, I was furious. I went straight to our house in Matthews and his mom, Lois was there taking care of them. I knocked and told her I wanted the kids. She shook her head -no. I found a brick, slammed it into the sliding glass door over and over. Then I took my children. Possession is nine tenths of the law, trust me. I had my babies back, but it cost me. He called an Emergency Temporary Custody hearing and told them I was crazy. He got temporary custody. But this was all a part of God's plan because now, people were watching him. Everything would eventually play out in a court of law. Now was my time to prepare for it. I knew Lois would take care of the children and he would be on his best behavior. I knew God was in control. I would have to rise above the storm. As the wind pushed me up higher, I gained confidence and strength. I wasn't afraid of anything except Ted and if I had to, I would kill him to keep us alive. Even though he had kids, he stalked me, called me non-stop, showed up at work, and had people follow me. It would only take one incidence to kill me, and he said he would. But

I felt a spiritual embrace more powerful than his words. God was with me, and I was so relieved to be away from him. In this time of protection, I started to plan. I had tried to plan before, but now my mind was free, and I could concentrate.

First, I took two extra part-time jobs and found the best attorney in Charlotte, William Brown. This was his last case before he would retire, and he took it because he believed in me and wanted to help me. Incidentally, when my mom was divorcing my dad, she was one of his first cases right out of law school. Now he was getting ready to retire and I would be his last case. Sometimes all it takes is one person to make a difference in your life and for me, he was that person. He instinctively knew Ted was a monster. I no longer had to have any contact with Ted and Bill stood up to him. Later we found out, he had attempted to hire someone to assault Bill but thankfully, no one took him up on his offer. They did, however, testify against him at our permanent custody hearing.

During the day, I worked at Volvo Finance, at night I waited tables at "The Fish Farm," and on the weekends I worked at a dog kennel. Bill said that I needed to rent my own house and have a bedroom for myself and Devin and Chase, so I did. It was in the University Area of Charlotte and my friend, Tina Johnston Smith, lived in the same neighborhood. This house was adorable, and I was never even there except to sleep. Bill documented Ted's refusal to give me visitation. All the free time I had, I spent in Ansonville riding horses with my dad. One night on the weekend, after finishing our shift at the Fish Farm, we all decided to drive to Mrytle Beach and watch the sun come up. It was so fun but, on the way back, we all still smelled like fish.

That year, I hardly ever saw Devin and Chase, but I knew this was what I had to do. The more he denied visitation, the worse it would look for him. Meanwhile I paid child support, and it came directly out of my Volvo Finance check. Working at the kennel was quite an experience but fun because I loved animals so much. I never knew why or how I had such a connection with them. They have always been a huge part of my life. But all this work kept my mind off things. Once at the kennel, I had to give a Rottweiler eye drop. Thank goodness, he was tied up. He snapped and attacked, I fell backwards to get out of his reach, and he only got my hand. When he bit it, it swelled the size of a boxing glove. Angels were with me that day. Sometimes they have a sense of humor. At the top of the grooming room, there was a huge blue sticky tarp paper that collected flies. One day, it fell on my head and swallowed me up. As gross as it was, I could not stop laughing. I waddled my way to a co-worker so they could laugh their ass off-I mean help me. I must have taken a shower and washed my hair ten times that day and still felt gross.

In an unusual way, The Fish Farm was a good place to work because I got free food and cash. It was very casual, just your local Fish Camp. I wouldn't exactly call myself a people person, but I could get what customers wanted before they could even speak. They didn't want to like me, but I was just so darn good. Bless My Heart! By then, I had years of experience waiting tables. Anywho, one night my friend, Sheila, told me that her boyfriend's friend, Greg, wanted to go out with me. She pointed him out and he was cute, and the opposite of Ted. His hair was blond, and he was good looking in a nerdy way. I had never been on a blind date before, and the permanent custody hearing was coming up. I needed to stay focused. That's when I heard a voice deep inside telling me to go and I did. Well, we really hit it off to say the least. He was intelligent, sensitive but also tough. Weeks later I got full permanent custody of Devin and Chase and overnight my life changed drastically.

I don't think Bill ever knew what he did for me and saying, "thank you," just didn't seem enough. Life was like a whirlwind after that. I started dating Greg, I had to quit my part time jobs, and Volvo Finance moved their offices to Texas. I got eight months' severance pay. I no longer had to pay child support and I didn't care if he paid or not as long as he left us alone. Of course, he had visitation, but it was limited. In trial, Bill provided witness after witness that stated Ted had offered them money to attack me, break into my home and kill me. He eventually went to prison for mortgage fraud and non-payment of child support. He got the money from Lois to get his child support caught up and never got behind again.

Me, Devin, Chase, and Greg moved into my mom's house. She moved into the condominium. After all this time, I felt like a warrior. I was now a majestic eagle flying high above the clouds. Like an eagle, I wanted a mate for life and when I married Greg, that's what I expected. I desperately wanted the family I never had. Michael had found it. He had the perfect little bible thumping family with the "smiley" wife and adorable children. He was a successful home builder; Christian family person and I was happy for him. He deserved it. Now, I deserved it too. **TURN THE PAGE**

CHAPTER 18 JUROR NUMBER NINE

At some point I realized, I was alone. My mom, dad and Don had passed away. Brandi was in California and Kerry was missing. Chase was in Asheville and Devin was in Florida. I only had Robin and Michael, but I was glad to have them. Technically I knew where Kerry was-in Norwood, but he was "hiding," so I gave him space. I didn't want to enable him, but I always checked up on him. I, myself, had been hiding from the world for two years trying to heal from unrelenting mental anguish. I wasn't just dealing with my own Post Traumatic Stress Disorder but also the pain of watching my mom, my dad, Brandi, and Kerry self-destruct. When the pandemic hit, I isolated myself from people, spent time with my animals, wrote and prayed. I wanted nothing to do with the outside world. I still watched the news and saw all the pain and suffering. It seemed as if it were happening on a planet far away. Then one day, during my bible study, I read the words that would change the rest of my life. I can't even remember the exact verse, but I got the point. If I continued to isolate myself, I wouldn't be able to fulfill my destiny and make a difference in this world. I didn't feel like I was ready to face the world again, but God whispered to me, "IT IS TIME."

I had received a notice in the mail for jury duty which I didn't think much about. I have received them before, and the notice tells you to call a number the night before to get instructions. Usually, I call, and they tell you that you don't have to go. But this time was different. When I called the recording, it said to be at the courthouse the next morning. Hmmm, how inconvenient. Now I would be stuck at the courthouse for a few hours. The following morning when I got to the courthouse, it was packed with people. There were about a hundred people there. It had been a while since I had been around people, and I felt anxious. The pandemic was over now but it felt strange. After waiting a few hours, we were all sent to a court room upstairs which reminded me of my classes at University of North Carolina at Charlotte. It was like a large auditorium. A well-dressed man stood before us and explained the "jury duty process." A while later another man came out and told us to go home and call the same number as the night before after five for further instructions. I was relieved as we all filed out to go home. With this many people, there is no way I would have to come back. But deep down inside, I knew. When I called, once again, it said to report to the courthouse the following morning. This time when I arrived, there were about half the people as the day before. We were immediately sent to court as the day before. The well-dressed man came out and said that if he called our name, we were to come and sit in the jury box. As he called the names, I was trying to figure out how this was going to work and then he called my name. I was startled but walked up to sit in the jury box and the number on my seat was nine. The prosecutor asked each of us question after question and some people were excused and replaced. Then the new people were asked questions. Again, people were excused and replaced. The prosecutor eventually stated that he was satisfied with this jury-WAIT, WHAT? But then, the defendant, who was representing himself, got to question and excuse jurors. I almost laughed, there was no way he would keep me, but he did. He excused three jurors and the process continued until he was satisfied. Then the name of two alternates were called and they were asked questions. The judge said, "this is our jury and the rest of you are excused from jury duty. My mind was racing. This was my duty, so I had to give it my full attention.

That day, I became the foreman on a murder trial. The trial began immediately. We heard the opening statement from the prosecutor and the defendant. Over the next several days, we heard testimony from an SBI agent, a police chief, and many other witnesses. Each of us had a huge "Juror" badge on because when we broke for lunch, no one was supposed to talk to us and we were never allowed to discuss the case, even with each other. There were many times we had to go to the jury room and wait so we slowly got to know each other. There was the lady that worked at the "Peaches and Cream" ice cream shop, the man that worked for the power company, a minister, two or three young people-each person was special in their own way. It was a good group; the court had done well. The last day, we heard closing arguments. The defendant, I will call "Ray," was a smooth talker and I knew from the evidence, although mostly circumstantial, he was guilty. I felt like this would be an easy decision and for eleven jurors, it was. After the defense rested, the judge gave me instructions and we were sent to the jury room. After we were seated, I told everyone that I would like to take an initial poll and then we could discuss the case in detail. I called out "juror number one" and they stated "guilty." As we got to me, I said, "guilty." I was thinking this may not be bad at all. Then juror number twelve said, "there is no way he did it," and we all gasped. She went on to explain her point of view and people began to interrupt her. We were all horrified that this man who shot someone in the back five times, could walk the streets. Day after day, each of us went back and forth with her. I would send a note to the judge asking to see different pieces of evidence. I poured over the evidence to find something new. His cell phone put him there at the scene of the crime. I asked her, "do you believe he was there?" She said, "yes, but that doesn't mean he killed him." We all looked at each other in disbelief. As I looked over the crime scene photos, I felt sick to my stomach. Then I remembered that I had to make a difference. People were getting frustrated, and tempers were starting to flare. It was 4:00, I sent a note to the judge asking if we could break for the day. That night, I kept going over the evidence in my mind to try and think of something we missed but we had discussed all of it in detail. I had no idea how to start the next day so when we all sat down, I looked at the minister and said, "if it's okay with everyone, I would like you to say a prayer." Everyone readily agreed and his prayer was beautiful. I felt at peace for the first time in weeks. One noticeably quiet lady started talking to juror number twelve for the first time. There was something about her voice that calmed juror number twelve. We all sat and watched as they talked back and forth. Juror number twelve sighed and said she needed some time to think, so I sent a note to the judge asking for lunch break. I noticed juror number twelve was crying. I told her no one was against her, and we all tried to make her feel comfortable.

As I walked out of the courthouse, I noticed the paint on the walls. It was original. This light cornflower blue color was the exact same that General Smith had used to paint every room of the mansion. This courthouse was a Neo-Classical Revival styled white building that was built in 1912 when the previous one burned down. The inside of it reminded me of the Titanic. The floors were all tiled, the ceilings were high, and everything seemed larger than life.

I decided to walk to a restaurant down the street to get out of the heat. I sat at a corner table and across the room was the judge and her clerks. I thought about the trial and knew it was a real possibility we would have a hung jury that day. God had asked me to make a difference and I guess I had failed. Before the civil war, the courthouse was a place where lavish parties were held in a ballroom. The court room where we were could have been that very ballroom. There was so much history in that courthouse and today we became a part of that history.

As we all arrived back in the jury room, everyone looked rested and a little sad. I looked over at juror number twelve and smiled. She said, "I'm ready." We all knew what that meant and I started filling out the paperwork and sending a note to the judge before she changed her mind. The lady that spoke to her that morning, Juror number seven, asked her if she was sure and she said that she was. The bailiff opened the door, and I handed him the manila envelope as we went to the jury box. The judge read the paperwork and asked me our decision. I said, "guilty." When the defendant asked to poll the jury, each of us were asked individually, was this your verdict and is this still your verdict? When it was my turn, I said "yes" and "yes." I tried not to look at juror number twelve, but I heard her soft voice say "yes" and "yes." I knew then, it was finally over.

We filed back into the jury room one last time because the judge wanted to thank us for our time. When the judge came in and thanked us, she asked if I was the holdout, and everyone laughed. One of the girls said, "you can't judge a book by its cover." The judge said but I thought I saw you crying. Someone else said she has allergies and asthma, which was true. Little did they all know, my tears were not for the defendant, my tears were for sweet little juror number twelve.

CHAPTER 19 THAT'S THE WAY LOVE GOES

Like a moth to a flame burned by the fire

My love is blind, can't you see my desire

That's the way love goes

Janet Jackson

I have to say this was one of the happiest times of my life. Chase, Devin, Greg, and I became a family. I suspected from the beginning that Greg was bi-polar. He had a terrible childhood, but he never used that as a crutch. Greg had two older half-brothers and he was the baby. When he was just a toddler his mother left and took everything except the kids. One of his brothers was in prison for murder. I never saw him or Greg's mother. His dad was in and out of prison and thank goodness, his grandmother raised him. I did get to meet his grandmother before she died, and she was a sweetheart. At first, he didn't have many depressive episodes and we got along very well. My depression was under control from medication and therapy, but he refused to take medicine or even go to the doctor. Greg was not only starting his own computer repair business, but he also built custom staircases. I got a job at Americredit-repossessing cars in the skip tracing department. Skip tracing means to investigate and locate vehicles and/or people.

Everything happened fast between Greg and I, we eloped on Christmas Eve and were back from South Carolina in time to have Christmas dinner with my dad. Every Thanksgiving and Christmas my dad would have a big dinner. After Christmas, it was Greg's birthday and then mine. We flew to Acapulco to celebrate our birthdays and our honeymoon. Traveling became a big part of our lives. After we settled down and gained about every pet you can imagine, the kids started doing well in school and we tried to take at least two vacations a year. Oh yeah, there was one more thing to celebrate, Greg and I were going to have a baby girl.

The problem was, since my blood type is O negative, I must get a Rhogam shot to prevent RH incompatibility. It worked the first two pregnancies but this time, it didn't work so I became a "high risk" pregnancy. If the baby's blood type was positive, my immune system could react to the baby's positive blood cells. Of course, Greg had no idea what his blood type was, so we began to panic. Most people have positive blood but fortunately when he was tested, we learned he was B negative. Just to be sure, (doctors had to be sure he was the father) I had to have an amniocentesis to draw the baby's amniotic fluids and test them. The baby had O negative blood just like mine.

Devin and Chase were excited about the baby and when my water broke, we all headed to the Matthews hospital to welcome Brandi into the world. Devin was born at Presbyterian Hospital and Chase was born at Carolinas Medical Center. When I was in labor with Chase, Ted took me to the wrong hospital, and I almost had him in the parking lot. I was in labor for two days with Devin and Chase just came right out. This labor was more like Devin's. In fact, my labor stopped and after waiting for hours, it had to be induced. At some point, the doctor realized that the cord was wrapped around the baby's neck. Brandi ended up healthy and beautiful and I requested the doctor to roll me straight into surgery to get my tubes tied.

Not only was Brandi a great baby but now I had Devin to help me with her AND, no more cloth diapers. Now there are disposable diapers, but they were expensive, so I used both. I had six weeks maternity leave, and I enjoyed every minute of it. Then something strange happened, Greg was going through some type of post-partum depression. One night he told me he wanted to commit suicide. I was angry. I felt like I had to take care of everyone. We had this precious, beautiful baby and now he wanted to leave us and this world permanently. It didn't make any sense to me. I thought he just wanted attention or was somehow jealous. I didn't believe him.

The next morning when I got up to feed the baby, (that was already sleeping through the night) Greg was gone. As I looked out the window, it was too dark to see how much snow we had. Schools were cancelled. It could have been half an inch, and the city would shut down. This was the South; I had my eggs and milk. One mention of snow and the grocery store shelves were empty, and all other businesses were closed. This time was different. As the light from the dawn grew, I could see we had about a foot of snow. The kids were already begging to go outside and play in it.

I wasn't worried about Greg driving in the snow. He had lived in Ohio with his grandmother, so he was used to driving in the snow and a good driver. I was worried that he left without telling me goodbye. Today he was supposed to be at Piper Glen building a customized staircase for a mansion. I looked at my phone and there was not a call or text from him, so I called him, and it went straight to voicemail. I shook it off and moved on. Breakfast was not going to make itself. After breakfast, I rocked and sang to Brandi as the kids were outside playing. Brandi and I already had a routine. Next was bathtime-her favorite.

When the house phone rang, I put Brandi in her crib and picked it up thinking it could be Greg. There are some moments in your life that haunt you forever. This was one of those moments. It was Carolina's Medical Center. The woman on the phone asked me if I was Michelle Blair and had a husband named Greg Blair. I told her yes as my stomach started to cramp. She told me that she was calling about my husband, Greg Blair. I needed to come to the hospital as soon as I could get there but there was no reason to rush. I said, "Why, what happened?" She said that she was unable to give me any details over the phone. I said, "Can you just tell me if he is alive?" She said, "as of right now, he is." She wouldn't tell me anything else. I called my mom to come and stay with the kids. I could not drive in snow and Cameros are low to the ground which makes it harder, but God was with me. I don't even remember the drive. As my mind raced, I thought he must have been in a car accident, and it was bad. When I got to the hospital and went to the front desk, shortly thereafter, a doctor and two nurses took me to a small room. They said some children were playing in the snow and found your husband parked in the woods. He had hooked a hose from his tail pipe into his truck and had carbon monoxide poisoning. He was alive for now, but they did not expect him to live. They had Greg in a hyperbaric chamber to try and reverse some of the effects. I asked to see him, and I followed them to another large room that was dimly lit. He was inside a glass coffin-like case with tubes going into his nose and mouth. There was a machine forcing him to breathe and he was struggling. I just stared. I asked the doctor how long he had been out there, and he said there was no way to tell for sure, but it must have been quite a while. He said that if the boys had found him any later, he wouldn't be alive. I asked him what I could do, and he said, "pray." Greg's dad and brother got there, and I left. I asked them to call me if there was any change. Honestly, I couldn't bear to see him like that. Besides, I was in shock. I couldn't process it. I knew Greg was getting the best care possible and I needed to be strong for the children. Before I left, I asked the doctor what were his chances and he said Greg had a 50/50 chance of making it. It could go either way. He told me to prepare for the worst and hope for the best. Days went by and he was still in a coma. One day when I got home from the hospital, I sat and opened the bible. I was crying. The children were with my mom. It was just me and God. I could feel the angels comforting me as I wept. I sat in the kitchen by the phone and read Psalms

23 over and over. I lost track of time. When the phone rang, I jumped and grabbed it thinking, "this is it; this is the call, he is gone." It was Greg's dad, Roy Blair. He told me that Greg came out of the coma and was going to be fine. When I hung up the phone, I had never felt closer to God. I had never been more grateful. We had been planning a funeral and now he had a second chance. I was overwhelmed with joy but at the same time, there was something about Roy Blair's voice that made me cringe. I didn't know it at the time but as I was sitting there with God, I was talking on the phone to a demon. **TURN THE PAGE**

CHAPTER 20 TAKE OFF YOUR GRAVE CLOTHES

Greg had to stay in the hospital for two weeks. When he got out, he wasn't the same. He was diagnosed as bi-polar with psychotic episodes. It felt as if Greg was raised from the dead and now it was time for him to take off his grave clothes and change his ways. I could tell he was trying. He needed to get rid of his old ways and work hard to please God, but Greg was an atheist. This was a problem. He didn't really have a moral compass even though he was a good person. In other words, he was Peter Pan. To him, it was okay to steal if it was for a noble cause-him. Who was I to judge him? The way he was brought up, I am surprised he was not a serial killer or Ted. I gave this issue to God because it was between him and God.

When Brandi was around two years old, we took the kids on vacation to the mountains, and I remember we had a wonderful time. Brandi was a loud and proud toddler so she and her "Barney towdel" dominated the room. She was in a playpen shouting and pointing as we brought our luggage in. Her first words were "shut up." She was so loud; we took her to get her ears checked. The doctor said she could hear fine; we just had a loud kid. Somewhere there is a video of this vacation, and it was a fun time. Even Greg seemed happy and stable.

When we got back, I saw a chance to buy a house in Albemarle, NC. It was a beautiful brick house with hills that were perfect for snow sledding. The house was in a nice neighborhood and the area reminded me of the mountains. Albemarle is within commuting distance of Charlotte and midway between Ansonville and Charlotte. After we moved there, I went to the Big Lick Festival (not dirty talk) -the festival was in the Big Lick community. Anywho, I bought a pot belly piglet and named her Charlotte. (later I got a male and named him Wilbur) We had a little tribe of animals and that was one thing I loved about Greg; he tolerated me. He loved animals too though. We had chinchillas, ferrets, a pig, a dog, cats, and an iguana. The neighbors hated us. Thankfully, we only had one neighbor. Chase and Devin loved the new house, and they made friends at school and in the neighborhood. Brandi even had friends at day care.

Greg began to concentrate on his computer business, and I went to work for Citizens South Bank as a collections manager. When I started, I never imagined that I would be there fifteen years and would eventually become a Vice President. My job consisted of working bankruptcies, collecting past due payments, foreclosing on houses, fixing them up and selling them. I worked with several attorneys, real estate agents and auto repossession agents. Most banks were losing money, but we were making a profit. My office was large and private, and I spent a great deal of time traveling to check properties.

Every morning, I stopped at Becky's Restaurant in Richfield to get coffee and breakfast. One morning while I was waiting at the counter to get my breakfast, I saw a newspaper lying beside me and I picked it up. It was the Charlotte Observer. When I opened the paper to read it, I locked my eyes with a picture of Benny Harris. It was the anniversary of his death and his family had placed a memorial ad there. Becky let me take the paper with me and tears rolled down my eyes as I wondered what might have been.

At work, I encountered so many strange things. Once I had to pick up a car that was owned by a man who had killed himself. I had just talked to him on the phone, and it felt surreal to drive his car knowing a few days earlier he had been at the wheel. I felt his energy and it was sad. I wondered if there was anything I could have done or said to help him. I told myself no matter what, I would never use my position to hurt people but to try and help them. Over the years, I stayed true to that, but I must admit, I became a little spoiled.

Whenever I first went to inspect a property, I could feel the energy inside the house. Ever since my Near-Death Experience, I had a sensitivity to the spiritual realm. The sadness and negative energy would try to take hold of my spirit, but I wouldn't let it. First, I would check for pets and people always left them, even goldfish. I always found them a good home. The goldfish went to a teller at the bank. Next, I would give the house a nickname like The Brady Bunch house, the Avon lady house, the dead house etc. The Brady Bunch house was decorated like the 1970's, the Avon lady house had a garage stacked with boxes and boxes of Avon all the way to the ceiling-she had passed away. And there were several dead houses-usually where something bad happened. Each house had a story to tell, and I tried to rewrite the story into a happy conclusion. Things don't always happen that way though.

After naming the house, I would secure and re-key it. Sometimes that meant breaking in and sometimes that meant dealing with angry people and/or dogs. I was careful but I don't know many people that would do the things I did. Once I gained entry, the cleanup would begin. You haven't lived until you've seen a refrigerator with rotting food that has sat there a year without any electricity. That was the next step, turning on all the utilities. I would have to check the house the day that it came on because people would leave water running and stoves on.

The first dead house was a house where an older man had died with his dog and the imprint of the dog was in the wooden floor. There was blood everywhere, but I had to focus on my job and not get emotionally involved. The guy that was with me to clean went outside to throw up. It looked like the man was eating breakfast, there was coffee still in the coffee maker and then something happened. I didn't know exactly what and I didn't want to know. The more I knew, the harder it was to focus on the job. That didn't stop me from getting to know the people from the energy. When people passed away, it was as if they were there with me telling me their story and this was no different. The man was lonely. His relatives forgot about him, but he had his faithful little dog that was always by his side. STOP. Focus. When I went down to the basement, I had to hold my breath. The smell was horrible. How would I get rid of this smell? I found the light switch and turned on the lights that had been off close to a year and there in front of me were shelves of creepy baby dolls. The man was starting to have some mental issues along with his physical health problems and there was no one there to help him. Stop. Focus. As the cleaning guy came down the stairs, I had to laugh. I knew he would have a shocked look on his face, but I wasn't prepared for the widening of his eyes and his hand covering his mouth. He slowly turned around and went back upstairs. I could hear him saying, "Michelle, this is the worst one ever! We're calling this the "dead babydoll house." When I finished a house and put it on the market, it was so rewarding to see the "before" and "after." I never put too much money in a house, but just took care of the basics. Cleaning and painting were always a "must." The energy changes when you clean up a house. It helps the spirits move on. Unbelievably, one of the worst issues was hoarding. For some reason, there were countless hoarders. It was either "goodwill" or "trash." I will say though, I'm still wearing Avon.

Greg and I took so many nice trips together. It was so great not to be in an abusive relationship. We had money and we used it. We went to The Canary Islands, Spain, all over the Caribbean, but my favorite family trip was Memphis, Tennessee. We saw Graceland, and the very first Titanic exhibit. It seems whenever things are going well, I expect something bad to happen. I didn't know it at the time, but this type of thinking affects your reality.

As Devin and Chase got older, they began to fight with Greg. Brandi could never do anything wrong. I always heard that. Chase and Greg were always butting heads and I felt bad for everyone. Greg no longer wanted me to have custody of Devin and Chase, after what I went through to get them back. Between that and Greg not believing in God, I felt we were doomed. I gave up on our marriage. If I had been patient and given this situation to God to handle, things may have worked out, but everything happens for a reason. When I decided to leave Greg, I was led by the Holy Spirit because it never occurred to me to go to my dad's ranch but that's where we ended up. He had five bedrooms; 2 bathrooms and this house had been home to many teenagers over the years. I felt like my dad owed me because he had not been there for me but seemed to be a father figure for all these other people. So, I told him me and the kids were moving to Ansonville to live with him and Faye, his third wife and last wife. I loved Faye, she was a sweetheart. Faye chain smoked as she cooked dinner, cleaned the house, and worked with my dad.

I remember my dad's frozen face as I told him we were moving in. No matter how hard he tried, he could not tell me "No." Deep down in my heart, I knew he loved me, but it was "deep down." Ansonville had always been on my mind. It was my security blanket. People could come and go but Ansonville was always "home." As I stood against a wooden fence post and looked out over the pond and pasture, the cows began to moo, and the horses began to neigh. I loved that sound. I even loved the smell. My dad let me bring all my animals because, well, he loves animals too. Change is scary but I felt secure at "The Ponderosa" as Kerry called it. I still had my job, my children, and Greg would always be a part of my life because of Brandi. I was led to do this, but I didn't know why. As I look back now, I realize, whenever I follow God's lead, there is a reason or purpose behind every move you make. **TURN THE PAGE**

CHAPTER 21 AGAINST THE WIND

Seems like yesterday

But it was long ago

Benny was lovely, he was the king of my nights

There in the darkness with the radio playin low and

The secrets that we shared

Mountains that we moved

Caught like a wildfire out of control

Til there was nothin left to burn and nothin left to prove

And I remember what he said to me

How he swore that it would never end

I remember how he held me, oh, so tight

Wish I didn't know now what I didn't know then

Against the wind

We were runnin against the wind

We were young and strong, we were runnin against the wind

And the years rolled slowly past

And I found myself alone

Surrounded by strangers I thought were my friends

Found myself further and further from my home and I

Guess I lost my way

There were, oh, so many roads

I was livin to run and runnin to live

Never worried about payin or even how much I owed

Moving eight miles a minute four months at a time

Breakin all the rules that would bend

I began to find myself searchin

Searchin for shelter again and again

Against the wind Little something against the wind

I found myself seeking shelter against the wind

Well, those drifter days are past me now

I've got so much more to thing about

Deadlines and commitments

What to leave in, what to leave out

Against the wind I'm still runnin against the wind

I'm older now but still runnin against the wind

Let the cowboy's ride They'll be ridin against the wind

Ride, Ride, Ride, Ride, Ride

Bob Segar

Don't cry because it's over, smile because it happened. There are things in my life I regret, and there are parts of my life I am immensely proud of. It may appear that some people have a perfect life. There is no such thing. People hide behind masks and put-up walls. Would I change my life? The answer is no because my experiences have made me who I am today. They have made me strong, resilient, forgiving, caring, generous and thankful. At times I have wanted to give up, but as my dad always said, "if you get bucked off the horse, get right back on."

When I moved to my dad's house, "The Ponderosa," it was quite an adjustment. I didn't know what always led me back to Ansonville. My roots there were so deep. Now I cherish this time I had with my father. We would go horseback riding every Sunday after church and dinner to get the cows up. Sometimes when I looked at him, I would see myself. It reminded me of the time I spent with Mama Gina and Daddy Jim. I remember the first time I saw my dad when he walked into Mama Gina's kitchen. I thought he was the most handsome man I had ever seen. He always wore a cowboy hat, jeans, boots, and a short-sleeved snap button cowboy shirt. Once I looked in his closet and it was full of these shirts and boots. But it was his personality, mannerisms and appearance that mirrored my own. We enjoyed watching game shows, playing cards, and talking. I grew so close to him that I could tell what he was thinking before he even said anything.

At first all the kids were there but after one school year, we realized the schools there were terrible. And Greg initially ended up getting custody of Brandi, just like Ted. It would be years before I got her back, and I would have to fight for her. Devin's grandmother, Lois, paid for her to go to boarding school in Asheville, NC at "The Asheville School." During breaks, she lived with Lois in Hendersonville, NC. Chase went down to Florida to work with his dad and finished school online.

As I looked out over the cow pasture, I felt a sense of peace. I thought they were all safe and following their destiny. Devin was safe but as I found out much later, she was the only one. How can I blame myself when I had no control? No matter what decision I made, it didn't seem like the right one. Once again, I worked all the time to save money for an attorney to get Brandi back. Even though now I was Assistant Vice President at the bank in Salisbury NC, I also worked at a nice restaurant in Albemarle NC and at night waiting tables. Albemarle, NC and Salisbury, NC were close to each other in location but the people were worlds apart. It didn't matter, I enjoyed waiting tables for a change of pace AND I got free food.

I guess Greg didn't want to make the house payments for the house in Albemarle because it burned down. I remembered that his dad had burned their house down when he was younger for the insurance money, so I figured he was behind it. I had to take a lie detector test given by the insurance company and Greg refused it. I passed, of course. He never filed a claim and no criminal charges were filed. It is hard to prove arson. It was so sad to see that beautiful house in ruins. I wish his dad had been caught and went to jail then. Our lives would have been without so much pain.

It seems when you can reconcile your relationship with your parents, you can truly begin to live. It happened with my dad, but it would take years before I felt that way with my mom. My dad wasn't perfect, but neither was I. My mom was a narcissist, but I didn't know what that was until much later. I researched it and learned what I needed to do in order to heal. I had to learn to put up boundaries with her. I had to learn to deal with knowing this type of personality disorder involves children prematurely in an adult world. Self-defeating thoughts and negative feelings are internalized over the years. I learned to block out traumatic events, but those negative thoughts were memorized. Feelings are masked as a survival mechanism. At some point, you must accept and grieve the mother you never had and never will have.

One weekend Kerry came to stay with us, and I could tell something was wrong. Him and my dad were whispering to each other. Kerry was sick and kept throwing up. Kerry lived in Greensboro, NC with his wife and children. He was a successful businessman, and I was proud of him. That day when I left to go to work, I looked up at the clear, blue sky and thought it had never looked so brilliant and vibrant. There was a cool breeze blowing and peace filled the air. When I got to work, I logged into my computer, and someone said to check the news. I pulled up the news coverage and there was a live feed. A plane hit the World Trade Center. I sat and tried to imagine how this could have happened. I thought back to a time long ago when me and a group of friends stood atop Tower 1 and looked out over the city of New York. Then another plane hit the second tower. This was not an accident. After hearing a plane hit the Pentagon and one was headed towards the White House, it was clear we were under some type of attack. I called my dad and he had heard already. All planes were grounded. I never really thought about seeing planes every day until the skies were completely empty. It was eerie. The bank had to stay open to show the strength of the nation. Everyone was calling their loved ones to check on them. They showed footage of people jumping out of the towers because they were burning to death. Phone calls from people stuck on the top floors were being played. They were saying goodbye and telling their families they loved them. The plane that was headed for the White

House crashed in a field. There were so many heroes that day. People on board that plane took control, firefighters were going into the towers when people were trying to get out. Then the first tower collapsed. Shortly after that, the second tower collapsed. People were running through the streets screaming. No one could breathe. It didn't seem real, as if I were watching a movie. I went home early. I just couldn't get any work done. My office was across from the bank so no one would notice. I was on salary and came and went as I pleased.

When I got home, Kerry was gone. My dad said Kerry's wife was having a mental breakdown and was going into a treatment center. That was Kerry's side of the story. When I heard the truth, I wanted to join her. Kerry had an affair with his fifteen-year-old babysitter and got her pregnant. The state was pressing criminal charges for statutory rape. So, what does Kerry do? He took Kevin's identity, strapped cash to his legs and took his family to Brazil to live. Thoughts of losing control can be irrational. I knew I had to give all my worries and anxieties to God. I gave God control and was attentive to his promptings.

Fear is a lesson learned, and I could have let it take hold of me, but I didn't. For the first time in my life, I was with my father, and I felt the presence of my father in heaven. One night as rain lashed against the sliding glass door, I gazed outside. The trees began to sway, back and forth. Their strong roots were anchored into the earth, like my roots were anchored in Ansonville. We would all face storms that would strengthen our character. I felt a strength inside of me like never before. My dad came up beside me and laid his hand on my shoulder. I wasn't used to seeing him without his cowboy hat. He said, "Is everything okay?" I smiled at him and said, "everything is just fine." In that moment, fear transformed to courage as I braced for the journey ahead. **TURN THE PAGE**

The
Koi
Pond

Kevin, me, and Michael/Me and Tiger

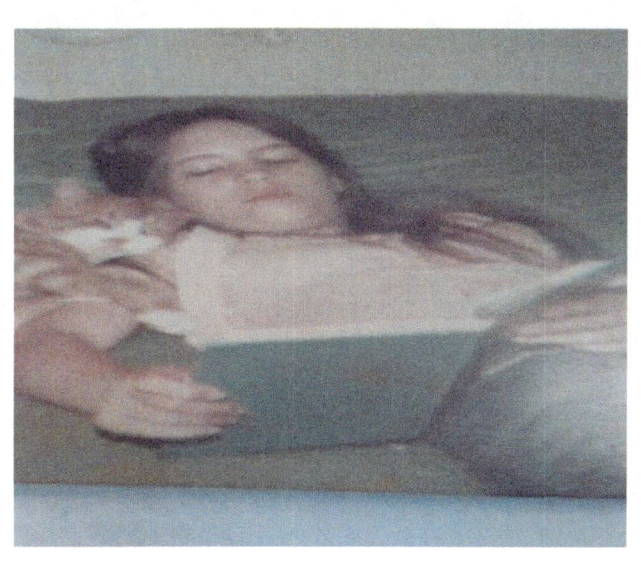

Riding my
first horse

Me and
Kerry

Me and Kerry/Me and Micheal

150

Mom and Dad/Mama Kate and her sisters

Jefferson and Nannie Martin-Mama Kate's father and mother

Seventh grade-our first concert-Styx-Charlotte Almond, Tanya Buff, me, Lisa Powell, Renee, Susan Hinson, Teresa Farmer

Me and Kerry/Softball team

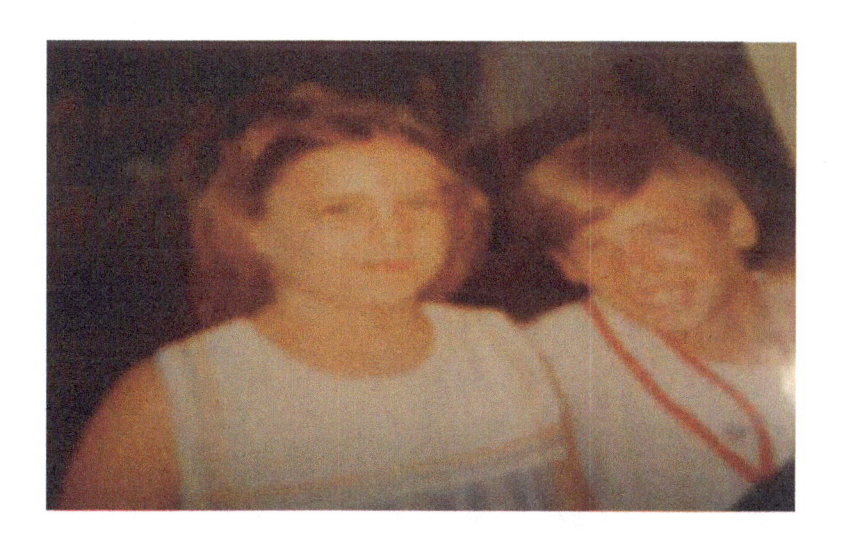

Me and Mark Brown

At JT Williams

Me and

Bonnie

Graduation-Myrtle Beach-me with hangover and me and Bonnie

Me and Benny

Robin, Michael, Mom, Me, Kerry, Kevin

Me and Sandra Wellman/Me and Devin

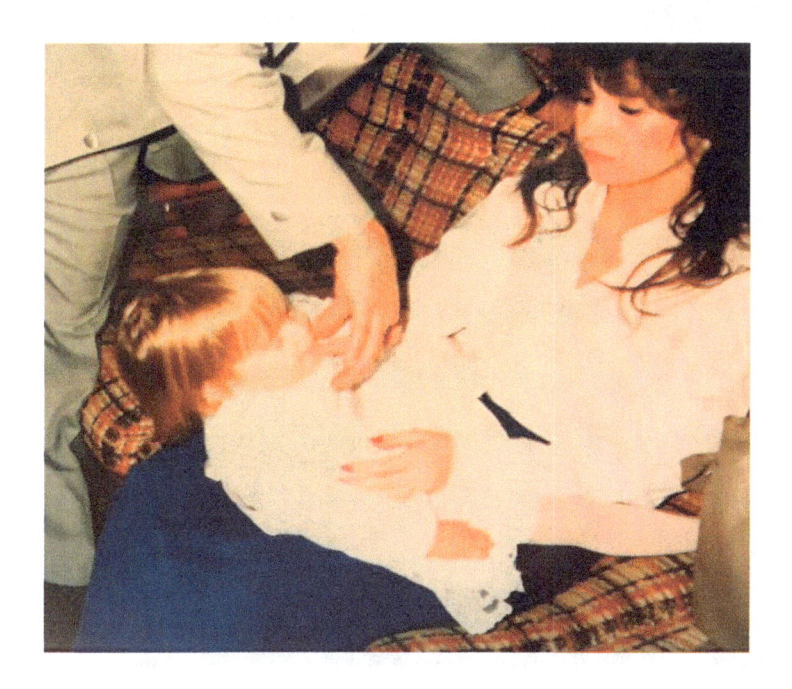

Chase

Brandi and Devin

Brandi and Chase

Lily and Primrose/Terry, Josie and Lily

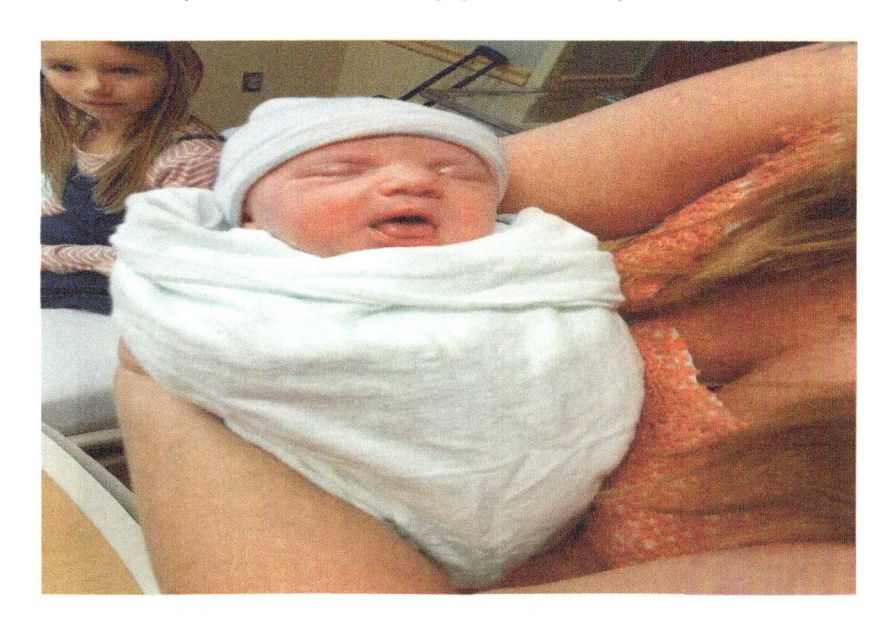

The Cottage

Bailey

Don's lights

Jacuzzi view

Plantation

Plantation

Mama Kate's House

Plantation pictures

Barn on the plantation

Chase and Josie

173

ACKNOWLEDGEMENTS

Thanks to **Greg Blair***, for helping me format this book! I appreciate your computer expertise. When I told you, "something on my computer is tearing it up," and you replied "yes, I know exactly what it is-'Michelle Blair'," well, you may have been right. Also, thank you for* **"our little black squirrel.***"*

Thanks to **Pastor Rodney and Danielle-** *for always being patient with me- (even when I didn't deserve it)-and for not being mad at me when I oversleep and miss church or choir practice. I love you both!*

Thank you to **Ethel Harris** *for giving me inspiration and healing! I'm so sorry I forgot my Christmas present at your house and never said "thank you." I was nervous and wanted to be part of the family.*

*Thank you to my brothers-***Michael, Kerry and Robin-**

I LOVE YOU!

*Thank you to my children-***Devin, Chase and Brandi-**

I LOVE YOU!

Thanks to **Jason, Jeff and Kate** *for loving me, being my support system and for giving me space when I needed to write!*

Thanks to **Janet, Lied and Stuart** *for being like family-I love you!*

Thanks to my forever friends **Carolina, Teresa, Christina, Sandra** *and* **Charlotte***, true friends like all of you are so rare-love you forever and ever. Amen.*

Thanks to all my animals-for your unconditional love and patience while I wrote!

AUTHOR BIOGRAPHY

Michelle Blair is an animal activist, avid reader, historian, and author of her first non-fiction book, **"Turn the Page: A Southern Chick's Memoir."** *Michelle earned her Bachelor of Science degree from Pfeiffer University where she graduated "Magna Cum Laude." After a successful career in banking and skip tracing, she went on to get her post-bachelorette diploma in Paralegal Technology. Michelle was a contract paralegal for a few years before starting to write. She is a board member for the Anson County Historical Society and has a facebook group called, "About Anson County." Retired and dedicated to writing, she now lives at "The Oaks" Plantation in Ansonville, NC*

Made in the USA
Coppell, TX
09 July 2024